New Voices, New Visions 2010
Essays from the Composition Program
Department of English

State University of New York at New Paltz

Edited by
Rachel Rigolino • James R. Sherwood • Joann K. Deiudicibus

Copy Edited by: James R. Sherwood

Learning Solutions

New York   Boston   San Francisco
London   Toronto   Sydney   Tokyo   Singapore   Madrid
Mexico City   Munich   Paris   Cape Town   Hong Kong   Montreal

Pearson Learning Solutions, 501 Boylston Street, Suite 900, Boston, MA 02116
A Pearson Education Company
www.pearsoned.com

Printed in the United States of America

1 2 3 4 5 6 7 8 9 10 XXXX 15 14 13 12 11 10

000200010270587182

CG

ISBN 10: 0-558-82768-3
ISBN 13: 978-0-558-82768-7

New Voices, New Visions 2010
is dedicated to
Dr. Pauline Uchmanowicz
Coordinator, Composition Program, 2006-2010
Teacher of the Year, School of Liberal Arts and Sciences, 2008
An inspirational teacher and colleague

Tom Olsen
Professor of English; Chair

Nancy Johnson
Associate Professor of English; Deputy Chair

Matt Newcomb
Associate Professor of English; Coordinator, Composition Program

Judges for the 2009-2010 Academic Year
Joann K. Deiudicibus
Mary Fakler
Penny Freel
Peggy Hach
Rachel Rigolino
Jan Schmidt
Ethel Wesdorp

Editors:
Rachel Rigolino
Joann K. Deiudicibus
James R. Sherwood

Copy Editor:
James R. Sherwood

Cover and Interior Photographs:
Morgan Gwenwald

NEW VOICES, NEW VISIONS
CONTENTS

Exploratory Essays

NEW VOICES, NEW VISIONS
CONTENTS

Informational Essays

Analysis Essays

NEW VOICES, NEW VISIONS
CONTENTS

The Exploratory Essay

Exploratory essays do just that—explore a topic that is of personal interest. They may be structured as a narrative or as a more traditional academic essay. The focus of the essay is not necessarily on the writer's life, but it can be. Examples of exploratory essays include autobiography, ethnography, examination of visual text, cultural autobiography, and reflexive autobiography.

My Life as a Camphill Child
Wietske M. Smeele

I walked up to the Starbucks counter where a woman wearing a green-and-white nametag bearing the name "Emma" stood. "One café latte please," I said. She scrawled my selection on a cup and, turning towards the computer, asked me for my name. "It is Wietske, W-I-E-T-S-K-E." I cringed slightly while spelling it; I hate giving my name. It and my accent always evoke so many questions. And, sure enough, the question came: "Where are you from Wietske?" I have never known how to answer this question because I have never truly known where I come from.

Ever since moving to America seven years ago, I have been searching for my true nationality. Sometimes I say I am English, sometimes I say I am Dutch, but I have never been satisfied with either of those answers. I was born in England, and lived there for the first eleven years of my life, though I am not English. It is your passport, a little book carrying your name, date of birth, and photograph, which pins a nationality on you. My passport is maroon, and on its cover, the word "Nederlanden" (the Netherlands) is typed in golden letters.

I grew up in the North Yorkshire Moors of England. My village lay nestled between the steep rocky slopes of the heather-adorned moors. But it wasn't until I was older that I realized the individuality of my little home-village. To my childish mind, it was natural to live in a large, three-story house with my parents, four siblings and five developmentally disabled adults. My village, Botton Village, is part of the Camphill Movement, a worldwide organization whose purpose is to create a wholesome living and working environment for adults with developmental disabilities. Volunteer families, such as mine, devote their home and time to these adults.

"Don't walk on my clean floor, Wietske!" Leslie called to me as, socks soaked, I jumped up and down on the wet kitchen tiles. Leslie was my favorite member of the household. She was a beautiful lady with Down Syndrome. She had cropped dark hair, a quick smile, and a rich

Yorkshire accent. For as long as I can remember, she had lived with us, pushing me in the pram when I was a baby and sharing in my tea parties. But now that I was six, she was my playmate. Every Tuesday, when it was time to wash the floor, I would run around the kitchen with Leslie chasing after me. And every Tuesday it was the same scene: me running helter-skelter through the house, shouting for Leslie to "come and get me if you can!" and Leslie calling after me that, if she were wearing her red jumper, she would be Lucifer and then I wouldn't be able to escape. Sometimes those afternoons ended in tears, sometimes in laughter. But no matter what the outcome was, I would always knock on her door to hug her goodnight.

When my parents told me, in 2001, that we were moving to Camphill in America, my first response was to ask whether Leslie would be coming with us. I couldn't imagine my life without my wonderful Botton family. But when I came to America, I realized that even though I did leave half of my family behind in England, I would always be able to find a new family as long as I was in Camphill. In Camphill Village Copake, USA, I met Katie. Katie is mentally unstable; she is an entertainer—a wonderful woman always full of life and laughter. Every morning when I come downstairs for my coffee, she starts laughing and crying at the same time, calling my name across the kitchen and asking for her "teddy-bear" hug.
"Chump-head, Wietske!" Katie called to me in her Manhattan accent from across the dinner table. "Where are you going tomorrow?"

"I'm going to New Paltz, Katie." I said.

"I'm gonna miss you sweetie." She sniffed; I would miss her too.

"Where are you from Wietske?" It was Emma, the Starbucks barista. I didn't hesitate this time. I knew that I wasn't going to say I am Dutch, or American, or even English. "I am a Camphill child," I said with a smile as she handed me my change. As I went to collect my latte I whispered it over and over again to myself: "I am a Camphill child." It felt right!

Heart and Soul
JANINE PIERANTOZZI

We often make connections between things and people who have affected us throughout our lives. Some of these connections are materialistic, while others remain in our hearts and souls forever regardless of what we have physically to remind us of them. When I was seven years old, my aunt started teaching me piano on her four-octave Yamaha keyboard, and I have been hooked ever since. Whenever I am stressed out, I can sit down and play for hours at a time, feeling like all my worries drain out through my fingertips and onto the black and white ivory keys.

 She was the "cool aunt," my favorite, and closest relative at the time. As my Mom's only sister, we could relate on the being the older sister, and she would tell me stories about her and my Mom when they were my and my sister's age. My aunt Wendy would always play the keyboard at her house and sometimes the piano at my grandma's house for me. I guess I started liking the instrument because she had played piano for years, and I wanted to be like her. One day, I told her that I wanted to learn, and with no hesitations, she started to teach me little by little.

I loved the piano instantly. She taught me new songs on her keyboard whenever I went to her house. I sat by her side as if from key to key. The first song she ever taught me was the classic melody of "Heart and Soul" that so many people who have ever played piano, even for a short amount of time, have passed on to one another.

After begging my parents to let me begin with private lessons, my aunt convinced them to allow me. The tables turned and I started playing for her as I avidly learned more each day. Whenever I saw her, I would practice to play her a new song, hoping she would be impressed and proud of me. She always was. I was doing well with my private lessons and my aunt and I remained close, as I grew older. From when I was born through my childhood and heading into my early teen years, she was there for every birthday, holiday, special occasion, or casual visit almost every week, even if it was for lunch at her house. I talked to her about everything and did not know what I would ever do without her.

It was around the second week or so of February, and my parents, sister, and I went ice-skating with my aunt and her husband. We all had so much fun together and I remember thinking that it had been one of my favorite days of that past year. It was the middle of winter and the ground was snow covered, without a patch of grass in sight. The cold air and chill of the wind wrapped around me like a vine on a tree branch, as the day that I never expected to come approached like rapid fire.

As my twelfth birthday was right around the corner, in that same month of February 2001, my sister and I were picked up after school by a family friend and brought to their house. I do not even remember why we were told we were going to their house for a few hours, rather than our own home, but I knew that something felt "off," as compared to usual. We stayed at our family friend's house for several hours until they drove us home, which I also thought was peculiar. It was pitch dark out when my sister and I arrived back home, and as I looked down the dimly lit hallway and saw both my parents on the couch, I knew something was terribly wrong. I felt a knot form into the bottom of my stomach before they even said anything and had never felt as nauseous in my entire life as I did then. My parents proceeded to tell my sister and me that my aunt had suffered from a brain aneurysm earlier that day. She was rushed to the hospital, but unfortunately, it was too late to do anything. I was overwhelmed by shock and confusion, losing someone who had been there for me in the hospital room, since the day I was born, and whom I thought would be there with me for much longer than the current point in time. Not really knowing how to deal with things, I continued to play piano and told myself that I always would for her, regardless of how much time went on.

Time passed, and I felt the obligation to keep getting better, taking lessons, and playing as much as I could. I felt that this was the only way that I could stay connected to my aunt. I did not have anything of hers, besides what she had taught me. I played everywhere and for anyone. I went to competitions and performances, and my music teacher worked with me on audition pieces for schools such as Juilliard and Oberlin. At fifteen, although I still loved the piano, I began to feel pressured by both my teacher and my parents. I had lost that original freedom and enjoyment to learn and play what I wanted to from my aunt. When I had played with or for her, I had felt no pressure; playing piano was my favorite hobby because my aunt was the one who had taught me how to play.

On my sixteenth birthday, my mom surprised me with my aunt's sapphire ring that she had always adored. I remember the thrill that filled me knowing that I had something of hers. However, it was now that I finally realized something. It was not that the reason for continuing to learn the piano was inconsequential, but I decided to love it—but not go to college for it or pursue it professionally. I was not happy taking lessons anymore. I decided that I loved the piano, but it was ok not to be a professional and to start playing simply for myself. I think that receiving something of my aunt's helped me to realize that what I had learned from her was enough and that I should not feel obligated to continue with lessons in order to remain connected to her. I finally felt a sense of peace and closure about her passing.

It took time, but I realized that I need no obligatory feelings to keep me connected to her. I became self-motivated to learn and now cherish the memories of where my inspiration to play originally came from. Thinking back to when I was seven years old, I know that regardless of where I am or what I am doing, she will have a special place in my heart and soul.

Stepping Off the Bus
AMANDA CZERNIAWSKI

"Do you want to play with my Barbies?" she asked, with wide eyes looking out from under her golden brown hair.

"Sure, but can I have the purple dress this time?" I pleaded.

"Yeah, okay but next time I think I should get it," she suggested. Jessica and I were best friends. As five-year-old girls, our ideal play date consisted of the game of "house" and Barbie dolls. Jessica and I grew up together and spent the majority of our friendship in her huge, windowless basement filled with endless amounts of toys. We were always together and we told each other everything. We had the basic components of an ideal, long-lasting friendship, or did we?

When we entered sixth grade, Jessica developed a desperate need to fit in with the "popular girls." Her new friend Rosa was short and curvy while I remained boy-shaped and curve-less. Rosa showed Jessica that boys were fun to flirt with while I persisted in the belief that boys had "cooties." She demonstrated how to apply just the right amount of lip-gloss to make your lips glitter; I thought makeup was stupid. Jessica began to wear skirts while I continued to wear my usual jeans and a t-shirt. Our views about life were going in drastically opposite directions.

Soon Jessica began declining my attempts to hang out. She made excuses, saying that she felt sick or had to run errands with her mother, but I knew what she was doing. I knew we were no longer as close as we had been. As it turned it, this was just the beginning of our separation.

It all began on a fieldtrip to the Maritime Aquarium. Side by side, Jessica and I walked toward the large yellow bus, with its tiny square-shaped windows. Her pink skirt flowed softly in the morning breeze. In spite of our recent problems, it was understood that Jessica and I always sat together; there was no question about it. However, this time she invited Rosa and her other new friends to join us. Three to a seat was never allowed, but Jessica insisted that we break the rules and have Rosa sit with us while her friends sat adjacent. For half of the bus ride, I sat staring out the window, watching the other cars go by. I was uncomfortable with the new addition to our seat and did not join in their sighs about the cute boys in the back of the bus. After a few minutes, it became very quiet, and I glimpsed over just in time to see Jessica whisper into Rosa's ear. It was easy to read her glossy lips as she stated, "She has yellow teeth and bad breath." I knew instantly she had been referring to me. Rosa shot her head my way and immediately burst out in laughter. Jessica's eyes narrowed as she glanced in my direction. Her eyes had lost their familiar sparkle; they were dull and emotionless. I could feel the tears building up behind my eyes.

I looked away in shame as I examined my smile in the window. I remember feeling the hardness of my teeth as tears streamed down my reddened face, thinking, "why would she say something so hurtful?" We were supposed to be friends forever. The seats of the bus had never felt so compact. I continued to hear their unbearable laughter and I couldn't control myself. The bus seemed to be collapsing all around me with no way out. I had never felt so betrayed. "Amanda, what's the matter." Jessica asked.
"Nothing, I'm fine," I blurted out. But I wasn't. I was far from fine. The feeling of being trapped made my stomach sick. All I wanted was to jump out of the bus.

When the bus pulled up to the aquarium's entrance, I rejoiced silently. I could not wait to break free from the compressed seats of my prison. My impatience was almost intolerable, but I did not want to give Jessica and Rosa the satisfaction of knowing they had hurt me. I wiped my tears and exited the bus, not looking back. "Where are you going?" Jessica shouted. I did not answer. To this day, I remember the image of Jessica standing there, with the yellow prison in the background, watching my back as I walked out of her life. The feeling of freedom was indescribable.

David Gemmel in Italy
IAN SAVITZ

As a child, I always dreamed that I had been adopted from some lost Baltic clan. I wanted to believe that my biological parents were warriors, sworn to protect their people but intelligent enough to know there was more to life than always fighting to survive. I thought that they tried to give me a new life, one where I could live and learn in a cultured world. My adoptive parents told me that my biological parents were Irish; they hoped either to crush my fantasies or to urge on my dreams to travel and reveal the secrets this world was hiding from me. While I am loath to give credit to my non-heroic biological parents, I must say that their abandonment left me with a spark that no rain could smother. My mysterious heritage became the focal point of my aspirations to travel, spurred further by the simple fact that I was adopted. I needed to find out where I belonged in this world, and I still have that need to this day.

From the time I first learned to read, I developed a strong interest in fantasy. I was the kid in elementary school who always read his book during lunch, preferring a fictional world to the real one. I read authors like David Gemmel and Raymond E. Feist, literary sculptors of whole worlds, even universes. Their books were so masterfully created that they needed a map at the beginning as a reference throughout the paperback fantasy realm. The more I read, the more my love for fantasy increased, transforming into a lust for existing in a completely different time and place. People who knew me well fondly stated that I "belonged in the realm of knights and swordfighters, when chivalry was a law, not a dead practice." I reached the point where I began to superimpose myself onto certain characters in the novels I read. Sometimes I was a 6'4" blonde giant of a man wielding an axe that shone like moonlight, even after the countless lives it had taken. Thieves and rogues were personal favorites of mine. Cunning and crafty, they controlled their surroundings perfectly, hiding in plain sight or in the shadows of a rancid, dripping sewer. While my character never stayed the same, my chimerical world always revolved around a time when fighting was a way of life, and laws were meant to be trod under chain mail boots. Reading left me with a yearning for a word that no longer, or maybe never, existed.

The vacations that I went on in reality were varied, and very disappointing in the beginning. The first time I ever left the United States was on a trip with my parents to London. As I descended the ramp from the plane, I held my breath waiting to see the world I had long awaited. I was sorely disappointed when all that greeted me was a smaller, less filthy version of New York City. The cultures I witnessed in England were surprisingly similar to those found in America, and the people were no more exotic than my Polish-American neighbors. Those images stayed with me through the whole trip, and I felt myself begin to lose hope in ever finding where I belonged.

A few summers after my dreadful trip to London, my parents again approached me with the prospect of going overseas on vacation. They had decided upon traveling to Italy, and while I was wary of another disappointment, I eventually gave in to their plans. Italy introduced me to a form of fantasy that I had lost hope of discovering. The experiences I gained in Italy left me with the heady feeling that I got whenever I delved into a particularly stunning novel. Instead of becoming lightheaded over a rogue with a dagger, I found a rush of emotion from a different culture, lifestyle, and language. People were more amiable and forthcoming. It was a freer existence, one that appealed to me greatly. There was almost a lawless feeling to it at times, when locals described to me just how nonchalant the police were about crime. It seemed the only law they ever enforced was the mid-afternoon siesta. The language was the last bit of distinction that I needed to feel like I belonged. Foreign languages flowed off the tongue like a river over worn pebbles. They are romantic and appealing, and they gave me all the excuses I needed to know that I wanted to travel the world.

While I lack foresight, I have begun to unravel a path for myself in the future. I have my goal in sight, and I found the first couple of stepping-stones. SUNY New Paltz gives students the opportunity to study abroad, to reform tunnel vision into a much wider perspective. I plan not only to enroll in the program, but also to spend as much time as possible exploring the world after my semester is through. With whatever money I save up, I can venture off on my own, and find my unique place. No amount of brainwashing in high school ever convinced me to let go of my dream. While everyone was worried about being accepted into a college to find a high-paying job, I was sure that I would find a way to achieve what I wanted. I stumbled upon the international relations program at SUNY New Paltz recently, and have been giving it significant thought. This course of study might be the means to the end for which I have been looking. Unfortunately, what exactly that end—that final place or idea that I have searched for all my life—is still unbeknownst to even me. I don't know what I hope to find, because deep inside I still dream of encountering my fantasy realms in some territory no one has ever explored. I expect that I will eventually decipher my own mind, and figure out what I need, and where I can find it. But until that day, all I can hope for is the opportunity to explore until I run out of shoes or land—whichever comes first.

I'm a Barbie Girl

Aruba Iqbal

Rebecca, a brunette with wide, chocolate-brown eyes, steps out of her bright pink convertible dressed in a dazzling burgundy gown. Her boyfriend puts his perfectly tanned arm around her shoulder in a display of affection as they walk together towards the large private jet headed for Hawaii. On the way to Hawaii, she changes her outfit three times. The stewardesses make sure to be as hospitable as possible in providing anything Rebecca needs. As they are preparing to land, there suddenly seems to be a problem with the engine and the jet plunges towards the ground in a spiral. Luckily for everyone, Rebecca knows how to pilot the doomed aircraft. She lands the jet with the finesse equal to that of a fighter pilot. Everyone exits the plane and Rebecca offers to take them all out to dinner after the scary ordeal. Sounds impossible, right? Not for Barbie dolls. In Barbie's world, anything and everything is made possible. Need a gown for the red carpet? No problem, just take a quick trip to Paris. Prom looming around the corner? Don't worry, longtime beau Ken is ready in his dashing tuxedo. Looking for a new career as a veterinarian? A professional chef? A teacher, lawyer, or rock star? No need to choose, Barbie can do it all! While Barbie was playing virtually every role possible in her world, she became a major icon in the real world and has had an important impact on our culture.

The idea of Barbie first came about from the desire to create a doll with an adult appearance for young children. Ruth Handler, known as the creator of Barbie, saw her daughter playing with paper dolls and putting them into adult roles ("Barbie"). At the time, dolls for young girls were depictions of infants and babies. With the new adult-figured doll, children were able to give their dolls more mature roles that could mirror real-life experiences. For instance, using a grown-up doll, girls could create make-believe weddings. Soon, all kinds of adult scenarios for Barbie were introduced. Girls were able to choose from an array of different occupations, houses, and cars for their Barbies as well as select friends and family members for her. As a child, I can remember wanting Barbie to be in high school one day, to having her be married with children the next. Because she was much older than I was, Barbie could do anything imaginable. My little "Baby Burp-A lot" doll didn't have those kinds of options. All she ever did was burp . . . a lot.

Although Barbie gained worldwide publicity, ultimately the doll became most popular in America. For this reason, hundreds of different Barbies were produced that appealed to American pop-culture and society, such as Elvis Ken and Priscilla Barbie and Malibu Barbie. Because of her fame, the song, "I'm a Barbie Girl" by pop-dance group Aqua became a hit; and Barbie dolls have also appeared in many movies, such as *Toy Story*. Current fashions are miniaturized for Barbie so that a child can virtually dress Barbie up like herself. During the time when "popcorn shirts,"—shirts with stretchy elastic scrunches—were a trend for teenagers, my Barbie, whom I named Rebecca, had a red and white one. I also remember being jealous of the shirt because hers was so much prettier than the ones in the mall. Provided with the latest fashions and accessories, Barbie became modern and adaptable. Barbie was able to go through the same fads and crazes that young girls went through.

Barbie's increasing popularity was also due to her diversity. The doll was made available with all sorts of skin, eye, and hair colors to provide an assortment of dolls to pick from and play with. By having this variety, children weren't bored with the monotonous appearance of their dolls. There was a doll for everyone, including a Barbie with a wheelchair. Barbie changed her appearance, clothes, professions, and even vehicles. She became a celebrity as a result not only of her fashionable clothes, but also of the songs written about her off-and-on-again relationship with Ken. However, just like any other celebrity, Barbie ultimately became the victim of controversy.

With the modern "body image obsession" sweeping across America, it isn't surprising that Barbie has become a target of critics. People began to complain that Barbie gave girls an unrealistic body image with her narrow waist, long legs, and large breasts. Barbie, some claimed, led girls into anorexia and other eating disorders. However, I believe that most girls do not look at Barbie and think about how they can attain her body. The truth is, playing with Barbies can teach girls all kinds of lessons, both big and small. For instance, I first learned how to braid hair by testing my skills on Barbie. By having a miniature model in front of me, I was able to see what I was doing as opposed to trying to braid my own hair. Also, in an attempt to make Barbie a unique one-of-a-kind dress to wear to her prom, I learned how to sew. At first I could not sew well, but by continuing to practice making Barbie's clothes, I was eventually able to make a skirt for myself. More importantly, young girls who play with Barbie are given the chance to play in the "adult world" and manipulate situations for themselves. If Barbie wants to go to the mall after school, she can jump in her red Corvette convertible. With a snap of her little plastic fingers, Barbie can become a doctor and save lives. Barbie can do anything she wants. This gives young girls the same message. If they want to be a pilot, teacher, doctor, actress, or anything else, they can do it.

Our contemporary culture has seen dozens of fads come and go, but none is more popular and lasting as the Barbie doll craze. After I stopped playing with my Barbies, I didn't have the heart to throw them out. Instead, they are somewhere up in my attic, probably throwing an election party or something. I can still remember the different situations I made up for them. Ken once confided in me that he wanted to take Barbie to the movies. I recommended my personal favorite, *The Little Mermaid*. Barbie decided she wanted a pet dog, so I helped her take the golden retriever, Ginger, out for a walk when it was sunny. I loaded eight of Barbie's friends up in her van and later, transformed the van into a picnic area for a barbeque. Life for Barbie was the way I made it, which was the point of the doll. Imagination fueled Barbie's world and gave her the legacy she has today. Like many others, I was a Barbie girl, in a Barbie world.

Work Cited

"Barbie." *Wikipedia.* 11 Oct. 2008. Web. 17 Oct. 2008.

Developing Jazmin
JAZMIN GILLIARD

During the process of personal growth and development, we have to go through major changes and challenges. Many aspects of a person define who s/he is and why s/he has developed in a certain way. Gender has a huge impact on identity development. It is the deciding factor of how s/he approaches life's obstacles, or at least that's the case in my experience. Even now, a little past my eighteenth birthday, I still feel as if it will be a long time before I will have a complete sense of who I am and who I want to be. Even so, I feel like I have developed a sufficient sense of self and a feeling of pride after going through my fair share of rejection, acceptance, confusion, and happiness.

In any family, expectations and restrictions make members feel suffocated and restrained; this is especially true for a girl in a large, semi-traditional Hispanic family. The head of my family is my eighty-four-year-old grandmother who was born and raised in the Dominican Republic during a time when women were not encouraged to continue their education after they knew how to read, write, and master basic math. Her hobbies and chores consisted of basic housekeeping duties; she cooked, cleaned, sewed, and tended to children. These were the skills that she was taught to value the most, and passed them on to her six daughters. Her sons, on the other hand, were encouraged to have fun and enjoy life to the fullest. They were not taught basic household duties; a man's job was to make money for the family that the woman must care for.

The Hispanic woman's place is pretty much established at birth. According to my grandmother, girls, at a prepubescent age, should know how to cook, clean, and tend to children. When my grandmother came to this country, she experienced culture shock. In America, women wore pants, did not cook, and lived alone, even though they were unmarried. For years, my grandmother encouraged me to learn how to cook and clean, while warning me not to wear pants and to act appropriately around boys. While I rebelled in many ways, my grandmother and aunts were especially upset by my decision to hang out with the boys. Apparently, associating myself with boys *no se ve bien*—it did not look good. Prohibitions against socializing with boys even included my male cousins. When I was seven, I was told that I could not play with my seven-year-old cousin because he was a boy. This did not sit well with me as I had plenty of friends at school who were boys. "Why is my family so different?" I would ask myself. As time passed, however, I began to understand the point of my grandmother's ridiculous restriction: one girl in a group of guys almost always will be perceived negatively. Even outside of my family's traditional culture, a girl who does this is often marked with a bad reputation. Yes, I have always been a rebel, but now I am considered one of my grandmother's favorites, perhaps because I have at least tried to understand her perspective.

In addition to sex, one's birth order affects the way a person perceives the world. As I have found, the first-born has the most confusing role and set of expectations. As the eldest, I am expected to set an example for younger relatives, and I am used as a guinea pig by my parents. As the oldest daughter, I was responsible for sharing mothering responsibilities, yet, I was not considered responsible enough to do many of the things other girls my age did. For example, I was not allowed to go on play dates or to sleepovers if the children's parents were not direct friends of my parents. Because I was always told that my little sister looked up to me and that I should set a good example for her, this meant that I was not allowed to date until I was seventeen years old. When I eventually was permitted a boyfriend, he was not allowed to visit me at home, as my parents considered my little sister impressionable. She might get "the wrong idea" according to my mother's reasoning. My dad's perspective on dating and sex was a curt, "Respect yourself." Although I often felt like a free babysitter and mother substitute, my experiences as the oldest child helped me to develop my own sense of responsibility and eventually gave me the strength to be independent.

As time has passed, I have learned to develop a better sense of myself, how to be a better Jazmin. A Jazmin who is proud of who she is. Now that I am in college and have left my sheltered life behind, I am excited finally, to have access to opportunities that will help me reach my full potential and challenge my developing sense of self.

Formaldehyde
CHLOË VOORHEES

The sheep heart's slimy, cold outer wall slid down my face, leaving a snail trail-like substance behind. I turned and mouthed the words, "WHAT THE F, KUNAL!" so as not to disrupt the quiet concentration of the AP bio class. I wet a paper towel and cleaned my face off at a nearby sink. As I returned to the lab bench, the heart lay lifeless on the dissection tray while Kunal slumped shamefully into his stool. Ignoring him, I put on gloves and began to cut a horizontal line from the right atrium down across the ventricles and over to the left atrium. The squeaking of an off-balance stool caused me to look up. Kunal leaned back and lifted two of the four stool legs off the ground with another loud squeak. "Sorry." The mumbled apology seemed genuine. I accepted the apology with a laugh. "It's okay; I love the smell of formaldehyde in the morning!" The funny part is, I really do love it.

The first time I smelled formaldehyde was an abrupt encounter. Walking into the science classroom on a brisk autumn day, an unforeseen rush of a humid stench hit my nose and mouth. The stinging heat overtook my senses. The formaldehyde became the only taste in my mouth and slowly crept down my throat into my chest cavity. "What is going on?" one of my fellow classmates coughed. "Dissections!" the new 10th grade biology teacher chirped. Goggles, aprons, and gloves were handed out. We laughed at each other's silly outfits and joked about squirting blood. Then the trays of withered, pale, fetal pigs were placed in front of us.

Appendages were spread and tied down, with heads tilted to the side or straight back. There was utter silence as I peered down into my tray. The entire room was still.

Before I knew what was going on a hand, *my* hand, was carefully running a scalpel over the neck, through the torso, and between the split legs of the pig. I tried to open the pig, and nothing happened.

The cut hadn't been deep enough. On try number two, I pressed harder. Little snaps and geysers of formaldehyde let me know I'd gotten through to the rib cage. The flaps of skin, tissue, and bone peeled back to reveal a mosaic of organs. The textbook images were of no assistance in identifying these organ parts before me. This was not colored ink on paper; this was once-living tissue that had been submerged in formaldehyde and hermetically sealed in a plastic freezer baggie. I spent the next 45 minutes in complete awe and bliss. I had my hands inside of an animal. I was examining a miniature and slightly altered version of my own body.

Ever since that first glimpse inside of the fetal pig I have been captivated by the human body. For a little while during every dissection, I ignore the hooves, paws, or beaks and pretend I'm looking at a human's kidneys, lungs, and liver. I try to imagine how it feels to look inside of a human, and eventually become stuck on the debate over whether I would be scared. Now as a freshman in college, I can't wait to begin dissections in my bio labs, and study the body in the giant lecture halls. Whatever I become, whether it is a surgeon, researcher, or professor, I know that the course of my education and life has been drastically changed because of that first fetal pig and my first whiff of formaldehyde.

Floating
JEREMY SIMMS

I spent much of my adolescence adrift amidst an archipelago. One isle was the jocks' domain. Another belonged to an enclave of artists. There was a cave full of musicians and a mountain summit bustling with partygoers. I would often land on one of these islands, only to set sail a short time later, discouraged and disinterested, for there was not one particular isle that completely satisfied me. This nomadic trend did not completely disrupt my focus, nor did it compromise my character. Instead, I was able to tour each isle without ever being truly involved. I was able to stick my hand in the furnace without being burned. I was able to discover who I was and what I stood for. But most importantly, I became aware of events and philosophies in my town, Roslyn, that perpetuated the lifestyle I had chosen, a lifestyle that was one of the ghost, the observer.

I suppose the first seed of my schism was planted back in sixth grade. I distinctly remember my social studies teacher harping about an "offensive" essay. It was written by a current male Roslyn High School student. In his essay, he blasted the frivolous nature and conformist attitude of the town. He wondered why "everyone" had a little white dog and a Mercedes-Benz (among other things). My teacher was infuriated at these stereotypes, especially since the essay had been published in a magazine. She said something like, "Well, now everyone's going to think that we here in Roslyn are a bunch of spoiled, self-centered assholes." Some of the students in my class were also riled up. It's funny, because as defensive and fanatic as they were that day, they were the ones that would soon perpetuate this stereotype. At the time, I was rather indifferent about the topic. However, subconsciously, my social awareness had become twice as keen.

From that point on, I began to realize that the controversial essay had contained some truth. At first, I picked up on little things, such as how half of the cars in the school parking lot were either a Mercedes or a BMW. Then, my observations became more substantial. I noticed, day after day, kids would leave their rubbish on the lunch tables. They would exclaim, "Someone will clean it up," or sometimes a real jackass would say, "I'm creating a job for the custodian." Some laughed. I was disgusted.

Compounding my frustration was the fact that the majority of these kids were about as well off as one could be. Even aside from the loving families and giant mansions, these individuals were generally intelligent and talented. To me, it was confusing as to why someone with immense personal strength and a sheltered upbringing would need to be so unforgiving and inconsiderate. At first, I tried to reason with myself, believing that this pandemic was simply a matter of immaturity. Sadly, this theory steadily lost credibility, as many of them remained egomaniacs even after they graduated. I then pondered whether human nature was involved. Was there a primal urge to feel superior? Did the students toss their garbage on the floor only because they knew there would be someone to sweep it up?

Admittedly, a dose of pessimism began to circulate through my veins. I became increasingly judgmental. It started with the cars. If a Mercedes Benz cut me off on the Long Island Expressway, I would have to speed up alongside it to get a look at the driver. Even before I caught up to the car, I'd have a list of the driver's probable attributes and a fictional pen ready to check them off. My list looked something like this: woman, blonde, wearing designer sunglasses, talking on a cell phone, and bonus points if she had that little white dog next to her in the front passenger seat. Gradually, this demeanor permeated my daily life, especially during school. I scanned the hallways with a superficial gaze. Abercrombie sweatshirt and plaid golf shorts? Probably a jerk. Gucci handbag and orange skin from a tanning salon in November? What a conceited, spoiled brat.

Even though I remained rather introverted, students and teachers alike took notice of my pessimism. For instance, my friends would often come to watch my volleyball games after school. When I would go up for a spike, I would often grunt after making contact with the ball. I didn't take much notice; it was just something I did to add a bit of drama and power to my game. Yet, after the match was over, my friends would circle around me. I'd almost always hear, "Simms! Why do you sound so angry out there on the court?" or "Simmsy! What's with all the rage, man?" These questions made me realize that the grunting was not just for show; rather, it was an expression of my anger. I began to realize that its sources were the judgments, stereotypes, and labels that I frequently distributed. I was looking at my classmates as if they were all horrible individuals when I didn't know a thing about them.

This realization about the level of my anger and pessimism came to light during a conference with my English teacher in junior year. During a break in our conversation, he pointed out a collection of dead insects resting up on the fluorescent light above us. He said, "Wow, look! There are about seven of them up there. Poor fellows." Almost immediately, I responded, "Well, if they didn't take a hint after having their wings singed off and their retinas fried, then they deserve to be dead." What came next was a phrase that caused a personal revelation. It was a phrase that showed me just how much of an extremist I had become. "Don't be such a Satanist," he observed. Initially, I was ready to laugh, but I quickly realized that he wasn't kidding.

At that point, I took a look around me. My pessimistic state of mind had blown me well off course. As I peered out on the horizon, solitude overcame me. There was not an isle in sight. There was nothing to observe anymore, and until I was labeled a "Satanist," I didn't realize how complacent I had become with the stereotypes I had created. It became clear to me that such a close-minded attitude produced nothing positive. Instead of floating, I found myself drowning, and given my situation, there was no one to save me but myself.

In light of my revelation, I slowly paddled back to the archipelago. I initially wanted to get as far away from drowning as possible. I wanted to land on one of the islands. However, within the first few weeks of my senior year, a voice akin to the author of that controversial essay reminded me that at one point, I had seen a real problem with Roslyn.

My government class was buzzing about their SAT scores as the teacher prepared her lesson. I stayed out of the conversation, as I didn't see a reason to shove my score in someone's face. A few students in particular were quite obnoxious and loud while exchanging scores. They sounded like ecstatic, bellowing walruses. Somehow, my teacher was dragged into the conversation. It wasn't long before one of the students asked how she did on her SAT, to which she replied, "I don't remember exactly. I'm sure I did pretty well, but the SAT is a standardized test. Why would you want to do well on a standardized test anyway? That just means you're good at being standard." Needless to say, the room fell into a deep, sustained silence.

From that moment on, I felt a true sense of belonging. I knew that I couldn't be an extremist, nor could I let pessimism control my actions. Yes, the residents of Roslyn did have their flaws, but becoming enveloped in criticizing the town and my peers would be detrimental to my character. However, most significantly, I knew that my place was out there in the shallows that separated the archipelago from the mighty sea, the gray area between total involvement and self-imposed exile. After all, to observe is to perceive, not to judge.

Suitcase Filled With Words

Paivi Grogan

Language is a journey. My journey began some thirty-eight years ago in a small town in Finland. Every summer my parents used to pack the car and take us camping in various sites across Finland. I usually shared the back seat with many of my elbow-sharp and loudmouth cousins. Nevertheless, going places was fascinating—an adventure to look forward to each year. The dialects people spoke were strange, funny and fascinating. Once we crossed the border to Sweden and were able to communicate with the locals with physical gestures rather than language. Somehow, by the end of the day we had food to eat and a bed to sleep in. I was awestruck.

After learning my Finnish ABC's, I found myself wondering how our neighbors learned language, as well. When we drove around Finland, I enjoyed all the sights, but I wondered what it would be like to live in each of those destinations, to go to school there, admire the same scenery every day, and speak with that strange local dialect. But I wanted to go farther. My parents were factory workers with very little money and education, so the only means for me to explore exotic cultures was through books and television. Imagination is a powerful vehicle. To fuel it, I read books and observed the world around me. I engaged myself with British and American TV shows with Finnish subtitles.

With the exception of few borrowed words, there are no similarities in the vocabularies of Finnish and English. The sounds and structures of these languages are also distinct. I loved the sounds of the English language. It was so expressive in contrast to monotone Finnish, with its long words and soft consonants. English grammar consists of complex rules, such as a specific word order, articles, prepositions, and gender, all concepts foreign to me. In Finnish, I can put my words in any order I please, and I don't have to care about articles because they simply do not exist. Prepositions do, but they function in a dissimilar way. I need to know how to "bend" my nouns in fifteen different ways to convey my message. This is not always easy, even for a native Finn.

After my journey through high school and college, I gained enough knowledge and courage to explore the world, finally. I packed my suitcase few dozen times. I learned my ABC's in English, Swedish, Spanish, French, and Dutch, and lived in countries such as Singapore, the Netherlands, and Ireland. It takes a lot of effort to learn a new language. Most of the time I've "talked" with my hands. While I may not have gathered many material things to drag around with me, my suitcase has been filled with words.

Putting down my heavy suitcase in a strange land and calling it home has been a learning experience, not only in language and culture, but also in understanding myself. I am a complicated person. I don't mean that I am difficult; I just have had a hard time understanding myself. I'm shy and reserved, yet I'm not afraid to sell everything I own and buy a one-way ticket to the unknown. I have a good sense of humor, but I cannot crack a joke. I can go through a brick wall, yet I don't hold the strength to carry a stone.

I have learned that I cannot run away from narrow-minded people. They exist everywhere. We are all very similar, except for our customs, traditions, and language. Language is the bridge that connects us. The journey we take defines our path (Lakoff and Johnson 91). It's up to us where we want to take our suitcases, and how we want to use those words we've stored up along the way.

I have now lived in the United States for eight years, with my roots solidly planted. I may have set my suitcase down for now, but I haven't stopped filling it with new words. Now, I am teaching my two-year-old son what it means to be Finnish-American. Last week he woke up with goop in his eyes, and he told me that his eyes were "broken." What an observation from a child with such a limited vocabulary! I hope he carries these words with him, adding more to his suitcase as he makes his own journey.

Work Cited

Lakoff, George and Mark Johnson. *Metaphors We Live By*. Chicago: University of Chicago Press, 1980. Print.

The Informational Essay
Informational essays, as the title suggests, provide information about a topic. However, in order to move beyond being merely descriptive, these essays include an interpretation of the topic under consideration.

The Afterlife Revealed
Lisa Pomerantz

Throughout time, people have disputed many metaphysical and supposedly unanswerable questions involving topics such as the nature of the world or the meaning of life. One of the most mysterious and mystifying questions is that of the existence of an afterlife. The threat of death can take hold of almost anyone, causing them to act in ways they never thought they would in order to avoid this deterministic fate for just a little longer. It has caused men to search ruthlessly for the Fountain of Youth, buy indulgences to escape the wraths of hell, and has turned friends against one another. The reason for all this chaos over death is the uncertainty surrounding the concept. Until now, humans have had no sure way to know what the afterlife is like or if there even is one. Today, science is putting forth efforts with the use of astral projection, or the out-of-body experience (OBE), and the near-death experience (NDE) in order to discover and record what the afterlife holds, and the discoveries will cause even the most devout atheist to stop and think.

Astral projection is "The nearly complete separation of consciousness from the physical body in a secondary vehicle" (Guiley 21). This secondary vehicle is known as the astral body, or "an etheric (spiritual) double that is the exact duplicate of the physical body" (Guiley 19). Many times astral projection occurs in one's sleep, yet the individual is unaware of its taking place. With practice, one can lucidly experience the OBE so that s/he will be conscious of him- or herself as s/he floats through the astral plane, the "plane of existence that lies next to the physical realm" (Guiley 21). The key to the afterlife rests within these astral planes, as OBE practitioners repeatedly report that they encountered the dead while astral traveling.

The NDE also gives insight into the world beyond the physical realm. The NDE occurs when a person is very close to death but survives, such as a cardiac arrest survivor. The NDE has been reported for centuries worldwide. It is common for one to report encounters with deceased relatives, seeing religious figures, a feeling of euphoria, and much more. It is believed that these experiences are the phenomena of an individual visiting the afterlife and being told that it is not her time to die and that she must return to the physical realm.

As Michael Shermer comments, "If we knew for certain that there is an afterlife, we would not fear death as we do, we would not mourn quite so agonizingly the death of loved ones, and there would be no need to engage in debates on the subject" (52). Shermer is right. We do not know for sure whether there is an afterlife, but that does not mean we are not trying to find out; in fact, we get closer to the truth each day. Great strides have been made in order to prove the existence of mystical beliefs of the soul and an afterlife. The OBE and the NDE have shed light upon the mysterious world of the beyond, providing evidence of its existence. The International Academy of Consciousness is just one of many organizations conducting scientific investigations with the use of the OBE, the NDE, mediumship, reincarnation research, electronic voice phenomena, spontaneous cases, and other avenues in order to research and educate the public on human potential, psychic abilities, paranormal phenomena, subtle energy, and self-development (David Lindsay 109-112). Projectiology is a new field of research that the IAC has developed. It utilizes astral projection in order to catch glimpses of the afterlife created from accounts of the subjects after astral travel. The OBE and the NDE are preferred over the other techniques of researching the subject because they are direct forms of investigation. Still, the OBE is most efficient as, unlike the NDE, the OBE is repeatable and the researcher can induce the experience upon his- or herself. In addition, the NDE is limited in that it is centered around a life review—meetings with deceased relatives, a revelation about unfinished business—whereas the OBE allows for deeper exploration of the afterlife as more experienced practitioners can begin to interact with the deceased and their environment (Lindsay 110-111).

Shermer makes the claim that all of these experiences are simply products of brain functions. He cites Andrew Newberg and Eugene D'Aquili's study which observed Franciscan nuns in prayer and Buddhist monks in meditation. During prayer and meditation sessions "their brain scans indicate strikingly low activity in the posterior superior parietal lobe, a region of the brain the authors have dubbed the Orientation Association Area (OAA), whose job it is to orient the body in physical space" (53). Shermer also cites neuroscientist Olaf Blanke's report in which electrical stimulation applied to the right angular gyrus in the temporal lobe of an epileptic woman brought about OBEs. To the scientist requiring solid objective evidence for the proof of any hypothesis, these seem like solid contradictions to the argument for an afterlife revealed through the OBE, although close inspection reveals that Shermer's claim is only partly true.

Mind and body are unarguably connected, therefore it makes sense that when a shift in consciousness occurs, the brain will react. This is clearly visible as the body does not function after death, when the soul leaves the body; there are no zombies walking the earth. Hence, it would make sense to say that when the astral body, or the soul, becomes partially detached from our physical bodies, that our mental functions will be affected in some way, and therefore it would make sense that mental activity decreased for the nuns and monks. The situation reversed in the case of the epileptic women, where the brain was affected and therefore it could be speculated that the electrical stimulation brought about a minor but genuine OBE. In debate with Shermer is Deepak Chopra, whose research supports the claim of the existence of an afterlife. Chopra cites a study in which "out of 344 cardiac patients resuscitated from clinical death" 18% experienced an NDE (56). These individuals were brain dead, and yet still able to recall this experience. Their souls had departed from their bodies, and yet they were still aware of events taking place. As Chopra says, "I rely a great deal on the possibility that mind extends outside the body. This is obviously crucial, since with the death of the brain, our minds can only survive if they don't depend on the brain" (56).

A close analysis of the cases Shermer cites reveal the differences among the sort of experience one will have during the OBE based upon one's mental state. Robert A. Monroe notes that "fear is the biggest barrier to being able to astral travel" (qtd. in Guiley), and experiences of OBE are not all the same. In fact, one can divide up the experiences into three categories or three levels. It would make sense to say that when one's goal is to astral travel deep into other planes of existence then they experience the least amount of fear or anxiety. As a result, these people will have the most profound experiences and can be placed at a level one. A level two experience is had by the person who desires an OBE but does not intend on traveling away from their physical body. A level three OBE is one where the person is forced into an OBE and does not know what is happening to her. This is the level of fear, while the other two are measures of intention.

Examples of level one experiences are those that the IAC studies, in which the subject purposefully ventures into the astral planes with a mindset desirous of discovery. Level two would be the self-induced deep prayer and meditation of the nuns and monks. These individuals do gain some insight during their sessions since they welcome the experience and therefore allow for certain sensations characteristic of astral travel, including a feeling of oneness or closeness to a god-like entity. This suggests that the self-induced OBE brings one closer to the astral planes of the afterlife than the forced OBE of level three. As James Allan Cheyne points out in his article "When is an OBE Not an OBE?" the epileptic woman's OBE was genuine, but she was reported as having been quite confused. Her experience was unexpected, and therefore it would make sense that she would be a bit nervous, or fearful, and would not attempt to explore other realms. In addition, if she did not know what she was experiencing, she would not know that there were other realms to explore, and would probably opt to stay as close to her physical body as possible.

It is extremely important to note that no subject in either one of the cases reported the deep exploration and experiences of level one OBEs used in the IAC's research. There was no claim of encountering the deceased, traveling to another plane, or any of the other experiences that have been reported by many astral travelers, who are not under the influence of any sort of hallucinatory drug and are not asleep and dreaming. Therefore, the prayer and meditation sessions and epileptic woman's experience, whether genuine OBEs or not, lack the distinguishing traits of those elaborate experiences under study by the IAC; they cannot be compared. Hence, if the OBEs Shermer cites do show to be false, this would not prove or disprove the genuineness of the IAC's OBEs. In conclusion, these cases are not definitive proof of the OBE being a real experience, yet they are also not strong enough arguments to claim that they are not.

Unfortunately, science is not advanced enough to record what occurs during an OBE, and therefore, all the information gathered is subjective. The reports are still valuable as they are validated by the reoccurring themes that present themselves in the experiences of different individuals. A report by John Belanti, Mahendra Perera, and Karuppiah Jagadheesan compared the NDEs of 300 individuals from ten different cultures: Africa, China, Germany, Hawaii, India, Israel, Mapuche, Native American, Netherlands, and Thailand. There were many similarities found cross-culturally, such as the presence of deceased persons or spirits in nine out of the ten cultures. Also, six out of the ten cultures contain experiences in which the person experiencing NDE did not want to return to his physical body but was either forced or coaxed back by other spirits. There are extreme differences noted in these experiences, such as the presence of a tunnel in one NDE, whereas in another there is no tunnel but rolling hills or a village. Many argue that these differences do not refute the validity of an NDE or OBE and that these reports confirm Lindsay's discoveries in working with OBEs, in which he found that some locations, generally those associated with spirits of the less advanced or recently deceased:

> interconnect with the physical dimension, taking
> advantage of the physical geography but being
> augmented by constructs of subtle energy [. . .] the
> building styles will be modeled on the architecture of
> the place with which the non-physical community is
> associated, and its people will tend to be from
> that culture, region, or society [. . .] On a parallel
> with these types of locations are ones where the
> common denominator that draws the inhabitants
> together is a shared experience in the physical
> dimension, or perhaps a shared ideology. (114)

Lindsay's discoveries explain the incongruence of the NDE across different cultures. It seems that, in the afterlife, the deceased gravitate towards what they were familiar with in life, so it follows that the visions of a NDE would also be composed of that which they are comfortable. An NDE could be quite shocking for the individual if they were unfamiliar with their surroundings.

The OBE and NDE are phenomena that will always have skeptics, but the evidence is more than thought provoking to even the most disbelieving. Each day more and more individuals have one of these experiences and add to the bulk of knowledge on the subject. Humanity would prosper greatly if science were to provide solid evidence of the afterlife/existence. This could give hope to many lost people, bring self-redemption to the evil, and bring together those who were once so frightened of the beyond. Man could live out the cycle of life and death with the awareness of the greater picture of the world, and in finding the purpose of life, humanity can evolve into a species of enlightened men and women.

Works Cited

Belanti, John, Mahendra Perera, and Karuppiah Jagadheesan. "Phenomenology of Near-death Experiences: A Cross-cultural Perspective." *Transcult Psychiatry.* 2008. 45. 121-133. Print.

Cheyne, James Allan. "When is an OBE Not an OBE?" *Skeptic* 38-41. Print.

Guiley, Rosemary Ellen. *The Encyclopedia of Magic and Alchemy.* New York: Checkmark Books, 2006. Print.

Lindsay, David. *Proceedings of the Academy of Spirituality and Paranormal Studies, INC.* Annual Conference, 2007. Print.

Shermer, Michael and Deepak Chopra. "The Great Afterlife Debate Michael Shermer v. Deepak Chopra." *Skeptic* 52-58. Print.

Farewell to Baseball's Vatican
MATTHEW D. O'NEILL

The room was dead quiet. Nobody dared to say a word. My friends and I sat there in anticipation and remembrance of what has always been a great part of American history: Yankee Stadium. Some of the greatest baseball players played in the famous white and navy blue pinstripes. For nearly a century, the pride of New York, the New York Yankees, have called Yankee Stadium home. Now, after eighty-five years and twenty-six world championships (the most in any sport), Yankee Stadium will be demolished. It will be a day baseball fans spend in mourning.

Yankee Stadium has been the stage for some of the greatest players the game has ever seen: Yogi Berra, Whitey Ford, Rich "Goose" Gossage, Joe DiMaggio, Lou Gehrig, Mickey Mantle, Alex Rodriguez, and the great Babe Ruth, just to name a few. George Herman "Babe" Ruth was quoted saying, "I would give up a year of my life if I could hit a homer on the first day of Yankee Stadium." Sure enough, The Babe blasted the first home run during the inaugural game on April 18, 1923 against the Boston Red Sox. From that point on, there has been nothing but a winning tradition for the Bronx Bombers.

The Yankees have won fifteen American League Eastern division titles and thirty-nine American League pennants. Of their thirty-nine trips to the World Series, the Yankees emerged victorious twenty-six times. One of the most memorable World Series championships came from the 1927 team, arguably the best team ever assembled in the history of the game. Nicknamed "Murderer's Row" because of the depth and power of the lineup, the 1927 Yankees won 110 games, and lost only 44. Led by Babe Ruth and Lou Gehrig, the Yankees scored 975 runs in just 154 games, and capped the season with a four-game sweep of the Pittsburgh Pirates in the World Series. This was the same year that Ruth set the major league record with sixty home runs during a single season; that record would later be broken by Roger

Maris in 1961 (61 homers), Mark McGwire in 1998 (70), and Barry Bonds in 2001 (73).

Not only have the Yankees been associated with a high-powered, star-studded offense, but they are also known for the most amazing pitching performance in the history of the game. On October 8, 1956, pitcher Don Larsen faced a high-powered Brooklyn Dodger offense that included Pee Wee Reese and Jackie Robinson in Game 5 of the World Series. On that October afternoon, Don Larsen did something no other pitcher in history has done: throw a perfect game in the World Series. He threw just "97 pitches on his perfect day, only once going to a three-ball count, that against Pee Wee Reese in the first inning. Reese then struck out" (Kindered). It was such a feat that after the game Dodgers owner Walter O'Malley asked Larsen for his autograph.

Now, greed has blinded owner George Steinbrenner. Beginning with the 2009 season, the Yankees will have a new stadium (still called Yankee Stadium), which will be built just across the street from where Yankee Stadium currently resides. The "new" Yankee Stadium will hold more people, ultimately bringing in more money for the money-hungry Steinbrenner, who has shown little loyalty to his players and coaching staff. This past season, for example, Steinbrenner offered manager Joe Torre a contract he knew Torre would reject. Torre turned down Steinbrenner and moved out west to coach the Dodgers. Another display of Steinbrenner's unfaithfulness involved one of his most loved players. Early in the season, catcher Jorge Posada suffered a season-ending injury. Instead of bringing up a catcher from the minor leagues, Steinbrenner acquired the best catcher in history, Ivan "Pudge" Rodriguez, at the trade deadline. Posada had been the starting catcher in New York for about seven years, and he was thrown aside, as if he was nothing. Steinbrenner has always been known throughout baseball as a man who cares about nothing but winning, and is willing to pay any price necessary to achieve that goal. Now, Steinbrenner has soiled one of the last three sacred ballparks in America.

Only three historic stadiums remain: Wrigley Field (Chicago Cubs), Fenway Park (Boston Red Sox), and Yankee Stadium. They all are the last original ballparks. Every other team in baseball has moved at least once in their history (excluding the 1993 and 1998 expansion teams). The Phillies moved out of Connie Mack Stadium; the Giants left Candle Stick Park; and the Dodgers demolished Ebbets Field and moved out west. Unfortunately, the Yankees are abandoning Yankee Stadium, leaving only Fenway and Wrigley as the last original ballparks.

The crowd was deafeningly loud yet reverent on this, the last night of Yankee Stadium as the former greats made their way to their positions. Pitchers Whitey Ford, Goose Gossage, and Don Larsen took the mound for the final time. The sons of the late Mickey Mantle and Joe DiMaggio honored their fathers by wearing their jerseys and standing where their fathers had stood those many years ago. I felt a rush of emotion come over me as Yogi Berra, now well into his eighties, waddled to home plate in the same dirty-white jersey he had worn back in the 1950s. One of the most beloved Yankees in history, Bernie Williams, took his final jog to center field and was greeted with a five-minute standing ovation. After the great players were introduced, the ceremony's finale was ready to commence.

Commonly referred to as "The House that Ruth Built," Yankee Stadium was christened with a Babe Ruth home run. In the true spirit of Yankee Stadium, the stadium that started with a Ruth, ended with a Ruth. To honor the great Babe Ruth, the Yankees invited his daughter to throw out the final ceremonial first pitch. Tears welled in my eyes as she was escorted to the mound, and delicately hurled the ball to Posada. I was deeply moved watching all these great players return to the place they called home for so many years. There is something about Yankee Stadium that instills an unexplainable awe in fans, and on that night, I sat there and shared in the silence and memories that was Yankee Stadium. Seeing all the fan-favorites and Hall-of-Famers was a powerful experience that words cannot adequately describe. It was marvelous.

After the hands of time were turned back that night, September 21, 2008, the stadium was electric with excitement as the Yankees took the field for the stadium's final game. Fittingly, the Bronx Bombers won 7-3 against the Baltimore Orioles. Once the final out was recorded, the team's captain, Derek Jeter, addressed the fans for the final time in the old stadium, taking off his hat and raising it to the fans in appreciation. As the fans reluctantly filed out, the lights were dimmed, forever laying to rest the greatest stadium in baseball history.

Work Cited

Kindered, Dave. "The Day Don Larsen Was Perfect." *The Sporting News*. 24 Feb. 1999. Web. 12 Oct. 2008.

The Town of the Foreigner
DREW M. HOSKI

Picture Ireland; what do you see? Shamrocks, Leprechauns, pubs, castles, rugged coastlines, Dublin? Sure, these are just a few of the aspects of Ireland that make it a worldwide tourist attraction. However, Ireland is not just a 32,599 square mile island consisting of little red-headed men scrambling for a pot of gold.

Ireland is divided into four provinces, each consisting of several counties. In the south of Ireland is the province of Munster, which is known for its Golden Vale, an area of rolling green hills and rich pastureland that is arguably the finest in all of Ireland. It is described as "a haven of beauty and tranquility" (Discover Ireland) with its never-ending hedgerows, breathtaking mountains, and lush forests. Ireland's Golden Vale is located on the borders of counties Limerick, Cork, and Tipperary, and here people live humble and relaxed lives.

Nestled in the Golden Vale is the small village of Galbally, in eastern County Limerick near the Tipperary border. About thirty miles southeast of Limerick City and ten miles southwest of Tipperary Town, Galbally is a picturesque village that sits in the Glen of Ahedow. The Glen is a secluded valley in the heart of Munster, which lies between the Slievenamuck Ridge and the mighty Galtee Mountains, Ireland's tallest inland mountain range. The moss-like mountains reach toward the sky in spring and summer. In winter, the sugarcoated peaks blend into the clouds above. Galteemore is the range's tallest mountain, exceeding 3,000 feet. On a clear sunny day, the view from the summit looks like heaven's blue sky has been sent to unite with the earth. For miles, one sees blocks of land in various shades of green and brown. Within these blocks are villages, castles, roving horses, pathways, bridges, rivers and forests. It's like looking out an airplane window, except you are one with the land rather than observing from a distance. Also within the Glen is the statue of Christ the King. Overlooking the valley, the statue blesses, with open arms, all who pass through the glen. People have different beliefs about the statue's significance; however, I see it as a welcoming gesture into paradise.

The village of Galbally is one of Ireland's hidden treasures. Galbally, or Gall Bhalie, means "town of the foreigner" in Irish. The name reflects the presence of English workmen who came to complete land surveys and remained to settle the surrounding areas of the village. Their families still remain. It is a small rural community of several hundred people who live life at a steady, easy-going pace. The church, shops, and pubs make it a typical Irish town, but Galbally sets itself apart from others. In 1994, the town won Ireland's overall National Tidy Town award, an annual award given to a town evaluated by its environment, tidiness, landscaping, wildlife courtesy, streets, and back areas. The multi-colored buildings lining the main road are like a rainbow, making the village a particularly pleasant and enjoyable place. In the center of town is a square with a statue of a soldier from Ireland's War of Independence (O'Sullivan). From the square's flower lined stone paths, the Galtee mountains poke their way over the village's buildings, giving an empowering view of what the heart of Ireland is like: rugged, yet beautiful.

History flourishes in the village of Galbally. Settlements within the area date back to around the thirteenth century, or perhaps even earlier, since the Vikings inhabited areas of Munster as early as the 9th century. The old Galbally graveyard lies just outside of town. A haunting yet majestic thirteenth-century moss-covered church is situated within the graveyard. In addition, there are two ghastly effigies, one of a man and the other of a couple. Little is remembered about the people honored by these haunting, life-like statues.

A little past the graveyard is the Moor Abbey, the ruins of a Franciscan friary built in 1471. Founded by Donach Cairbreach Ua'Briain, it has a long history of violence and destruction. There were attempts to burn the structure in 1472 and 1569, and in the 1570s, three monks of the community were murdered inside ("Moore Abbey"). Despite its past, the Moor Abbey is an elegant structure that has brought renown to Galbally. The moss growing on its ageless stone walls has made the abbey even more beautiful. Walking through the arched passageways is like taking a step back into medieval times, being engulfed by the tunnels of time-worn stone. From a distance, you can see the large rectangular tower reaching towards the sky, dotted by little windows through which monks would once be seen. A large oak situated next to the structure creates a dramatic effect; in the spring and summer, the sprawling branches drop their leaves at the foot of the abbey. Leafless in the colder seasons, the oak provides a chilling and eerie feeling, as if it were growing out of a gothic novel.

Galbally is in some ways a typical Irish village and in others not. It's green, it's old, and has pubs. However, Galbally is different in that it is not a popular tourist destination such as Dublin or the Blarney Stone. This small town provides a true taste of rural Irish life, and that is its charm. Visitors to Ireland should remember that true beauty is not always found by scratching the surfaces of expected places. Rather, it exists in the hundreds of small towns and villages scattered across the island.

Works Cited

"DiscoverIreland.ie/Tipperary." *Failte Ireland*. National Tourism Development Authority, 2008. Web. 9 Oct 2008.

"Moore Abbey." *Archdiocese of Cashel and Emly*. Archdiocese of Cashel and Emly, Web. 2 Dec 2008.

O'Sullivan, Jim. "Galbally, Co. Limerick." *Beara Breifne Greenway*. n.p. 2003. Web. 12 Oct 2008.

The Issue of Immigration Illegality
JAMES R. FISCHER

Picture the day of an average middle class American citizen: s/he awakes early for work, seeing the children sleepy-eyed but happily off to school, and comes back home for dinner with very little fear or concern for the future. This is the clichéd American lifestyle. Now picture the trauma one would endure to find that this world was suddenly a living and breathing nightmare: the streets filled with wreckage and debris, the distant sounds of screams and gunfire growing ominously louder . . . or perhaps there is simply nothing but fallow land, scorching heat and the prayer that one's family will persevere through another day without food. This is reality for many who immigrate to the United States. The harsh and merciless landscape of their home countries causes them to flee their homes in order to preserve the well-being of themselves and their families. For those interested in the struggles of these immigrants, one can easily find films, books, and articles that investigate their stories. Three interesting perspectives on the subject are: Carlos Sandoval's and Catherine Tambinis's documentary *Farmingville*, which depicts the lives of immigrants in a Long Island suburb; *Crossing the BLVD: Strangers, Neighbors, and Aliens in a New World*, in which Warren Lehrer and Judith Sloan present their readers with a collection of narratives about recent immigrants; and Matt Ruslings' article, "Sierra Leone's Amputees," which delineates the struggle of those emigrating from a war-torn country to the United States.

The documentary *Farmingville* depicts both views of a bitter controversy between illegal immigrants living and working in the Farmingville community and those who are opposed to their presence. A central issue on which the documentary focuses a great deal on is whether a center for day laborers should be constructed with taxpayer dollars to avoid hate crimes as well as to reduce the fears many citizens have of day laborers. A woman, who helped found the Sachem Quality Of Life organization, is seen throughout the documentary conveying the fears and concerns of the general public against illegal immigrants. "I couldn't believe they called me a racist," she says after campaigning against the construction of the center. In her view, illegal immigration is detrimental to society in terms of the decreasing number of available jobs and the fear and anxiety people face when passing a group of immigrants on the street. However, she does not seem to understand that many of these immigrants are not residing in her town by choice. Many Mexican immigrants are driven from their homes and families by Mexico's economy. They come to places such as Farmingville and undertake the most arduous—and in some cases dangerous—jobs available. Construction companies are often in dire need for such employees. These men use what money they need to sustain them in the United States, and send the rest back home to their families. For many immigrants, the United States is a last resort in their quest to attain economic stability.

Poverty is not the only motivation driving immigrants over our borders. For others the threat of death hangs close overhead and sanctuary can be found only in fleeing to a foreign country. Ideda Antosi, or Bovic, as he refers to himself in *Crossing the BLVD,* found himself in such a predicament when he was forced to leave his home country of Zaire. From "1965 all the way to 1997, Mobutu Sese Seko was president of Zaire" (Lehrer 78). Bovic describes his rule as a decline from general popularity to the establishment of a military dictatorship casting the nation into a civil war. Bovic who had ideologically been opposed to the Mobutu government joined the Union for Democracy and Social Progress, a movement against the dictatorship that would brand him as a revolutionary and an enemy. Bovic in order to support his family accepted an offer by the government to work on the water network. "[He] never wanted to work for the Mobutu government but [he] did want to provide the population with drinkable water [as well]" (Lehrer 78). Bovic was indeed trying to help better the situation in his country but after refusing to join the military under a newly established law, Bovic was discovered as a UPDS member and was forced to leave his country and family by the threat of death. It is only reasonable that a man in Bovic's situation should be given amnesty in the United States. Ideologically it may seem to some that his obligation was to stay and promote the movement for reform in Zaire. However, the fact that he is a solitary individual who could do far more alive than dead goes overlooked in such an opinion.

Victor Saidu, an immigrant from Sierra Leone, lives now in Chicago. His home country being devastated by the Revolutionary United Front (RUF) uprising forced him to flee his country and he was no longer able to support himself after the amputation of both his hands: His ear was also cut off by a child soldier about twelve years old..." (Rusling). He said, "I was leaving everything, I was leaving my home. You cannot take nothing with you. You are going to a different land but you don't know where you are going" (Rusling). Saidu, with his disability, could no longer stay and work for the betterment of his country. To do so would not help resolve the issue but certainly end in his death. Saidu fled to the United States where he was provided with prosthetics and physical rehabilitation, as well as janitorial and other skill training to help him survive in the United States. "The conflict, which ended in 2002, displaced two million people, or one third of the population" (Rusling).

Immigrants are for many reasons justified in entering within the United States, whether legally or illegally. The situation is not as black and white as many would believe. Those who break our laws are no different from any other criminal and should be treated justly, but for those who seek simply to survive, and are furthermore willing to assimilate themselves within a new society to support their families and or countries, it is only humane to embrace these individuals.

Works Cited

Farmingville. Dir. Carlos Sandoval and Catherine Tambini. Camino Bluff Productions, 2004. DVD.

Lehrer, Warren, and Judith Sloan. *Crossing the BLVD: Strangers, Neighbors, and Aliens in a New World*. New York: W.W. Norton and Co., 2003. Print.

Rusling, Matt. "Sierra Leone's Amputees: A Refuge in Chicago." *Immigrationhereandthere.org*. The William and Flora Hewlett Foundation, Jan. 2008. Web. 1 Nov. 2009.

Community Service: A Help or a Hassle?

KELSEY A. ANDERSON

As a requirement for my Composition II course, I had to complete three hours of community service. The purpose of this assignment was to encourage students to become active in their community in some way. I thought that the volunteer experience might be both interesting and educational. As I had had experience volunteering at both my high school and church, I thought that finding community service would be an easy task that I would enjoy doing. However, I discovered how difficult it was, in fact, to find a community service site that wanted my help.

Over a three-week period, I searched unsuccessfully for a place to volunteer. I started by calling the types of organizations that I knew took volunteers: soup kitchens, a homeless shelter, a nursing home and an elementary school. All of them were located in Poughkeepsie. I was shocked to learn that none of the sites needed or wanted volunteers. The soup kitchens and the shelter told me that they were booked with plenty of volunteers until late June but would love the help then. The nursing home and elementary school told me that they could not allow people from the community into their facilities unless they were trained and certified or related to a resident or student. I then began to call and visit places within the New Paltz community. My first stop was the Family of New Paltz, which is organization that helps homeless people in the area. Once again, I was turned away.

After seven attempts to volunteer my time, I began rethinking my steps. Over my four years in high school, I had completed almost a hundred hours of community service. I had never found it difficult to find a place that needed volunteers. I then realized that because I was not part of a community service organization or club, volunteer work can be difficult to come by. So, I attempted to join the community service club on campus, Circle K, and found that they do small projects for the community but do not really go out in to the community to volunteer on a regular basis.

Eventually, I was able to find a job working at the New Paltz Youth Program (NPYP), which is a place where adolescents from New Paltz can go after school as a way to stay off the streets and out of trouble. As a member of the New Paltz Community, I have heard people call the young kids that walk the streets in New Paltz after school and on the weekends, "Gutter Rats." I do not exactly know where this term came from. However, I did ask the older couple I heard talking about "Gutter Rats" what they meant by it. They explained to me that "Gutter Rats" are the young people that walk the streets making trouble and stirring up the community. I was very excited when I contacted Jim, the director of NPYP. I have always had an interest in working with adolescents and this was the perfect opportunity to find out about the "Gutter Rats" of New Paltz.

NPYP is meant to be a teen hangout that provides a safe environment where, when they need it, teens can seek assistance from adults whom they trust. The house has been remodeled into a recreational space for teens. Scattered about the building's two floors are an air hockey table, a pool table, four computers, two big screen televisions, two video game systems, vending machines and many couches. The atmosphere is welcoming. During the time that I worked at NPYP, sixty adolescents, ages eleven to seventeen, signed in between 2:30 and 5:00 p.m. The adults who work at NPYP see themselves as both role models and friends to all of the kids who come and go.

The center was completely different from what I had expected. Instead of having organized activities and structured programs, NPYP allowed the teens to have their freedom. The teens that came to NPYP could come and go as they pleased, and they could do whatever they wanted to within the facility. Granted, there were ground rules, but there was no structure. At first, I thought, "This is going to be like a zoo," but to my surprise, the teens were well behaved and polite.

When I first arrived at NPYP, I was very excited, but also a little uncomfortable. For the first forty-five minutes, I was nervous about interacting with the teens because they all seemed to be comfortable among their friends. I had been told to observe them and to make sure that they were following the rules and having a good time. At first, I simply walked about, analyzing the differences among the adolescents in the building. I caught myself classifying the kids into groups with stereotypical labels such as "punks," "skaters," "goths," "gamers," "athletes," and "loners." Suddenly, I realized what I was doing. I was labeling people without even getting to know them. I then sat down and began talking to the teens in order to peel off the labels that I did not want them to have.

I discovered that the majority of the teens at the center were males. The boys had broken themselves up into about eight separate groups while the girls seemed to have divided into six or seven groups. A few kids were not in any group and sat by themselves. In each of these groups, the kids talked about the same basic things: how their day at school had been and what they planned for the weekend. As long as no one from a different group tried to enter into their conversation, they interacted well together. I noticed that when the kids who were by themselves tried to involve themselves in the group conversations, they were not readily welcomed. There was usually some remark such as "mind your own business" or "get lost." I decided to target these teens.

I asked the five kids who were by themselves if they wanted to play a board game with me. They accepted my offer with hesitation. They all thought that I was a new kid at the program; they did not realize that I was volunteering. When they asked me what I was doing there, I told them I was just checking out the program and volunteering. It was funny to watch their shocked reactions to this news.
As we played the board game, we talked about their ages, hobbies, families, and friends. Hearing them talk helped me to break the stereotypes that I had formed earlier. The four girls were twelve through fifteen, and the boy who played with us was twelve. Over the course of the next few hours, I was amazed to learn about their talents. As it turned out, each of them participated in a range of activities such as singing, dancing, karate, skateboarding, gymnastics, track and drama.

By talking to these five individuals, I learned that they were the younger kids at the program on that day. They all attended the New

Paltz Middle School, and they all had older siblings who were also at the Youth Program. When they told me that they had older siblings there, something clicked with me as to why these very friendly young people were not "in" a group. They did not want to associate with their older brothers or sisters and their older siblings did not want them in their group.

The youngest of the girls thanked me for playing the board game with her. She gave me a big hug and told me that she normally hated going to NPYP after school because she would sit on a couch and read by herself the entire time. She asked me if I would be coming back, and I told her I did not know. She was a little upset because she said that I was the only one who had ever tried to include her. I told her that she had friends there and could always count on the older girls (who were trying to comfort her) to have a good time and include her there. She then hugged me again and said, "I guess I never realized, thanks for your help and I hope to see you again."

This interaction made the whole experience of trying to find a volunteer site worthwhile. I was touched that I had helped this young girl feel included. I had wanted to place labels on the different groups of adolescents based on their appearances, but by watching and interacting with the different groups of teens at NPYP, I also came to realize that they are all individuals who just want to be recognized for who they are. Service is valuable because it not only helps others but it also teaches the volunteer. In the fall, I hope to return to the New Paltz Youth Program to continue my work.

The Analysis Essay

In writing an analysis essay, the author examines a text in order to reach an interpretation or conclusion. Examples of analysis essays include book, music, and film reviews as well as the more traditional literary analysis paper most of us have written in English class.

Transformations: A Poet's Search for Meaning
ELLEN HASPEL

Anne Sexton had a unique voice, unique for her time and unique for the material that she chose to express her deepest feelings of loneliness, disappointment, and sorrow. In her book *Transformations,* she looks at the revered fairy tales of our collective childhood and creates brilliant new stories by filtering the tales through her own personal difficulties with being a woman in the mid-twentieth century. Through her beautifully articulated pathos, she infuses life into the stories that have no doubt been watered down and oversimplified through the ages. To read these poems now is enlightening in several ways. The initial impact of reading the classic tales that she rewrites with such irreverence to the original stories is quite liberating; it opens us up to a new world of interpretation and enjoyment. As we continue to read, we are able to experience her deeper expressions of rage, irony, and disillusionment. Anne Sexton's strongest feelings are most evident in three of her poems: "Briar Rose," "Cinderella," and "Snow White."

In "Briar Rose (Sleeping Beauty)," Sexton presents the relationship between Briar Rose and her father the King as one of sexual abuse:

> Little doll child,
> come here to Papa.
> Sit on my knee.
> I have kisses for the back of your neck.
> A penny for your thoughts, Princess.
> I will hunt them like an emerald.
> Come be my snooky
> and I will give you a root (16-22).

Sexton may be infusing this poem with feelings about her relationship with her father, who was said to have sexually abused her (Wagner-Martin). If so, Briar Rose is no longer an archetypal princess but something more real. She is a survivor with scars and frailties consistent with her childhood trauma. In the Grimm Brothers' version of "Briar Rose," the King seeks to protect his daughter from danger of the curse that looms over her (Grimm). In

Anne Sexton's poem, the King is the perpetrator of the harm being done to his daughter. Even after Briar Rose is awakened after her hundred-year sleep by a kiss from her prince, she remains traumatized by her father's sexual abuse:

> Briar Rose
> was an insomniac . . .
> she could not nap
> or lie in sleep
> without the court chemist
> mixing her some knockout drops. (100-106)

Briar Rose's sleep is a metaphor for the denial of her father's abuse. It is a state of numbness Briar Rose employs to deal with the horror of her experience. She cannot live happily ever after as she is expected to. She has become damaged goods:

> Each night I am nailed into place
> and I forget who I am.
> Daddy?
> That's another kind of prison,
> It's not the prince at all,
> but my father
> drunkenly bent over my bed,
> circling the abyss like a shark,
> my father thick upon me
> like some sleeping jellyfish. (148-156)

Perhaps Sexton turned to drugs or alcohol to help deal with her own feelings after being abused. This poem may have been a confession from her, a way to make real what happened to her, to speak about the unspeakable. Growing up and finding her own prince did not erase her pain and disillusion. She still felt like a prisoner.

In "Cinderella" we sense a more lighthearted approach to this rewriting of the fairy tale. Yet, the story still centers on another central female figure who must endure certain hardship and rise to overcome her troubles by finding and marrying the prince. This plot point is again supposed to cure all that ails the leading lady, but sadly, it does not. It only gives her a different set of circumstances to navigate. The tone of this Cinderella is very sarcastic. One can almost picture the narrator of the poem spinning this modern version with a cigarette in one hand and a dry martini in the other:

> You always read about it:
> the plumber with twelve children
> who wins the Irish Sweepstakes.
> From toilets to riches.
> That story. (1-5)

Cinderella wants to go to the ball in the hope of finding a way out of her grueling scullery-maid existence—in other words, to find a husband. Now there is the ultimate irony! In fairy tales, newlywed princes and princesses have an enormous staff to cook, clean, and attend to every unpleasant task. In the real world of 1971, when these poems were written, a new bride generally looked forward to completing these odious jobs herself. In fact, that perception has not changed significantly in modern times. Today, although a vast number of married women have full-time careers, most are still the primary caretakers of their family and household. They have laundry, cooking, shopping, cleaning and child rearing to look forward to when they return home from long hours at work each day. Who needs "Prince Charming?" How about "Prince Equal Household Responsibility," or "Prince Let Me Do That For You Honey," or even "Prince I Can Wash My Own Smelly Underwear"? Anne Sexton's dry observations in the last stanza of the poem clearly illustrate her disdain for the fairy tale image of marriage:

> Cinderella and the prince lived,
> they say, happily ever after,
> like two dolls in a museum case
> never bothered by diapers or dust,
> never arguing over the timing of an egg,
> never telling the same story twice,
> never getting middle aged spread,
> their darling smiles pasted on for eternity. (96-103)

It is clear that her own experience of married life was nothing like Cinderella and the prince's image of perfection. "That story" is a lie.

The third fairy tale heroine I would like to examine is Snow White. In Sexton's version of "Snow White and the Seven Dwarfs," Snow White is a thirteen-year-old virgin. She is painted as a delicate doll, with "cheeks as fragile as cigarette paper, / arms and legs made of Limoges / [. . .] She is unsoiled. / She is as white as a bonefish" (3-4 and 12-13). Snow White is on the verge of womanhood, a dangerous place for an innocent girl. Her virginity and her great beauty have tremendous value in this poem, as youth and beauty are seen as important, yet temporary, commodities for all women. This point is made even clearer by the jealous Queen, who perhaps was once as beautiful as Snow White but has since withered and aged. Yet, the Queen's worth in her society and her vanity demand that she still be declared the fairest in the land. She cannot relinquish this powerful position. And so she commands that Snow White be put to death. When that does not happen, she disguises herself and relentlessly tries to kill Snow White through poisoned laces, apples and combs. This only slows Snow White's rise to power, as a freak coffin accident retrieves Snow White from her poison-induced coma, thus ushering her into the hands of the prince who has fallen for her while she has been assumed dead: "As the prince's men carried the coffin / they stumbled and dropped it / and the chunk of the apple flew out / of her throat and she woke up miraculously" (130-134). It is interesting that Anne Sexton does not include the magical kiss in this poem. But no matter, the prince ushers Snow White into the land of sexuality and marital bliss. The old Queen is forced to fade into oblivion, implying that as a woman ages, she loses value as she loses her beauty. The mirror which so many women turn to in search of validation can only reflect the outer appearance and not the inner self. I find it strange that the vast majority of women's magazines published today still do not subscribe to the belief that a woman's true worth is found in her character, intelligence and capacity for compassion.

Literary critics have said that Anne Sexton's *Transformations* is a milestone in feminist literature. Considering the era it was written in, I would have to agree. *Transformations* garnered rave reviews when it was published, and most critics agreed that Sexton had fused confessional poetry with professional craft (Litz 689-690). Yet there is also an underlying feeling of defeat to these poems. The author's tone implies that there is real doubt as to whether the conditions she is bringing attention to will ever improve. Unfortunately, Anne

Sexton took her own life before she could see some of the many improvements the feminist movement brought about for today's women. I think that if we look at how her poems have shone a spotlight on some of the difficult conditions that have challenged women through the ages, we can clearly see her contribution as an artist. The road she illuminated is a road we are still traveling on, still trying to find our true value, and still rewriting our own life scripts.

Works Cited

Litz, A. Walton. *American Writers: A Collection of Literary Biographies*. Vol. 2. New York: Charles Scribner's Sons, 1981: 689-91. Print.

Sexton, Anne. "Briar Rose (Sleeping Beauty)." *Transformations*. New York: Houghton Mifflin, 1971: 107-108.   Print.

Sexton, Anne. "Cinderella." *Transformations*. New York: Houghton Mifflin, 1971: 97-98. Print.

Sexton, Anne. "Snow White." *Transformations*. New York: Houghton Mifflin, 1971: 9-10. Print.

Wagner-Martin, Linda "Anne Sexton's Life." *Modern American Poetry*. University of Illinois at Urbana-Champaign. 17 Nov. 2006. Web. 23 Apr. 2009.

Define "Normal"
Traci Daubman

By any rationalization, outward appearance is hardly an indication of an individual's character. Whether one is physically beautiful or has deformities, a person cannot be fully understood without a look into his personal life, experiences, or inner disposition. Among the most physically unappealing individuals, many have vibrant inner beauty. Katherine Dunn developed such characters in her novel *Geek Love*, characters who challenge the inept definitions developed by society to distinguish normalcy from freakishness.

While the physically grotesque and deformed are seen by society as freaks, more often than not, those with apparently normal outward appearances mask ugly character traits beneath appealing physical façades. Early in the progression of *Geek Love*, the reader is introduced to a seemingly normal individual with a corrupt inner core. Vern Bogner is a man in turmoil. With his wife divorcing him and children who despise him, he turns to alcohol to heal his tribulations. Upon initial sight of the Binewski family, a family whose members are "freaks," a drunk and angry Vern fires several rounds of his gun into the backs of these innocent but unsightly "things." Vern fails to cause any significant harm to any member of the Binewski family, which is yet another example of his failure. Dunn revives Vern's character several chapters later where he has a more influential role in the lives of the protagonists. As his life continues to deteriorate, Vern Bogner's seemingly dull outer surface succumbs to the hideous character living within. Kidnapping his children and murdering his wife in a final attempt at accomplishment, Vern finds himself again a disappointment as a failed suicide attempt leaves his face badly disfigured.

The character of Vern gives the reader insight into the criminal minds of those defined by society as normal. With his outward appearance more closely resembling those he once viewed as freaks, he is forced into a state of guilt and remorse for the crimes he has committed and devotes himself to work for the Binewski carnival. Even as he responds to Arty's every need and writes the most innocent words to the family, the dark side of this corrupt individual has not vanished with his appearance and slowly begins to resurface as the plot progresses. Teaming up with Arturo in order to achieve his goals, Vern commits the most degrading act imaginable to his character as he attempts and accidentally succeeds at raping Elly and Iphy. Even in his most corrupt moment, Vern remains aware of his guilty conscience as he begins his encounter with the twins: "he just came in slowly, kind of bobbing and bowing apologetically with every step" (Dunn 253). It is this final cowardly act that reveals Vern Bogner's inner character as a dark and demonic individual whose corruption cannot be erased by the portrayal of a guilty conscience. In his own recognition that the sexual encounter is not mutual, the Bag Man, as he becomes known, writes remorsefully, "If you would rather kill me, it will be O.K." (Dunn 253). It is characters such as these that formally challenge the definitions established by those in the communities in which the Binewski family encounters, and allows those once viewed as grotesque to shine above those with apparent normal qualities.

It is not uncommon throughout the discourse of the novel for those with ordinary appearance to feel a sense of lacking within them. Dissatisfied with their everyday lives, masses of people reveal that they would rather succumb to a cult following than defy the odds on their own. As defined by journalist Norval Sanderson, "Arturism is a quasi-religious cult making no representations of a god or gods, and having nothing to say about life after death, therefore representing life itself as offering earthly sanctuary for the aggravations of life" (Dunn 227). Those within this cult-like religion are screened for admission based on several qualifications, charged a four-figure dowry for admittance, and most notably, agree to have one or nearly all limbs and body parts removed. A deformed individual himself, Arty leads this cult, encouraging all others to devote their lives and bodies to living more closely to him, thus providing him with the money and power he desires. In his attempt to create a larger interest in admission, Arty establishes a list of those to be excluded from the possibility. Convicted felons, those accidentally mutilated and those over the age of 65 are among those excluded for the reasoning that they are considered already to be freaks in Arty's eyes (Dunn 228). The acceptance of such policies and regulations by seemingly normal individuals again provides the audience with the realization that freakishness and corruption come from within all types. With a seemingly normal outward appearance, it takes either courage or desperation to allow one's physician to remove all of one's limbs, thus dramatically and permanently influencing one's lifestyle. This physician in particular is no exception to the rules as she has her limbs amputated and her brain lobotomized by the willingness only of Arty himself. This interaction among the characters poses as one of the most significant symbols of Dunn's plot. The individual making the incisions is, in time, added to those among the Arturian cult against her will, therefore proving that no individual will be cast any higher in rank than Arturo himself. This relationship further challenges the role played between the norms and the freaks as the definition becomes blurred.

With pride at the core of the family, protagonist Olympia Binewski exudes a foreign sense of confidence as she encounters several individuals who wish to display her disfigurements. It is her encounter with Miss Lick, the owner of a strip-club-type atmosphere for the disfigured, that reminds Oly how blessed she is to be the individual she is. An unsocial but normal and successful woman, Lick exploits those with physical irregularities and creates abnormalities within those wishing to be admired on her stage. Similar to Dr. Phyllis, Lick allows those dissatisfied with their ordinary lives to become something bigger. Becoming a distinguishable and common theme throughout the plot's progression, there appear to be more normal individuals seeking disfigurement than disfigured individuals attempting normalcy. Pride appears notable in the Binewski family and those within their carnival. As they exhibit what they have been born to accomplish, their society around them attempts to imitate their deformities. The relationship initially formed between Oly and Miss Lick is altered as the plot thickens. Lick seemingly seeks a relationship with Oly which she has not anticipated. As Lick relates how similar they are with their orphan-like status and secret families, Oly reveals the similarity that lies within their common simple desire for someone to talk to. In her recognition of their differences, Oly states, "The only point where our narrow tracks converge is her bid to turn my darling into one of hers" (Dunn 340). It is at this point in the plot where she begins to question Miss Lick's incentives and their relationship in its entirety. Despite their ever-changing relationship, the comparison between normalcy and freakishness becomes too much to handle for Olympia as she resorts to taking the life of Miss Lick as well as her own. While they exuded similar inner beauty, the differences in outward appearance and their impact upon their friendship were such that could not be revoked. It is in this manner than the Binewski family challenged the societal definition of normalcy at its peak.

While society is limited to the constraints of the pages of a fictional novel, the definitions provided by those individuals do not define those of deformity as freaks but those who can seek alternative means to beat the odds and choose to become like the extraordinary. With the common ability to mask their inner corruption, it is those who lack the courage to face their challenges that show their true colors. It is the subtleties of true freakishness that can potentially be detrimental to one's character, despite an outwardly normal appearance.

Work Cited

Dunn, Katherine. *Geek Love*. New York: Vintage, 2002. Print.

Darkest Before the Dawn
ISAAC B. GETLAN

In his 2003 hit song "Tip Drill," rapper Nelly laments:

> I need a freak (Ooh) to hold me tight,
> I need a freak for 7 days and 7 nights (ooh),
> I need a freak (ohh), that will not choke (ohh),
> I need a freak to let me stick it down her oooooh (99-104).

As vile as these lyrics are, there are even more shocking examples of the trend away from hip-hop's roots that has been occurring for over a decade. As each year passes, it seems that mainstream hip-hop becomes more commercial and pointless. Hip-hop today has become, for the most part, a violent and misogynistic genre of music, but many artists are trying to keep the original ideas alive. Artists like Lupe Fiasco, Common, Kid Cudi and others keep the focus on political and social issues within African-American communities and America as a whole.

Violence has been a constant theme in hip-hop, but only since the early 1990s have hip-hop artists advocated and celebrated it. Hip-hop's violent history can be traced back to the foundation of gangsta rap, with artists like N.W.A, DMX and Notorious B.I.G. (Chang). One of the early examples is N.W.A's 1998 song "Fuck tha Police," in which Dr. Dre holds a mock court case over the Los Angeles Police Department's brutality towards minorities. Although this song is not primarily about violence, the testimonies that Ice Cube, MC Ren, and Eazy-E rap express their anger at police brutality and racism in very violent terms (N.W.A).

Today, many rappers rap exclusively about detailed ways to hurt people. One of the most repulsive examples is Marshall Mathers, the rapper known as Eminem. In his 1999 album *The Slim Shady LP*, Eminem raps about killing his wife and drowning her in a lake and encourages a man to kill his cheating wife and her lover (Eminem). Despite these themes, *The Slim Shady LP* stayed on the Billboard

200 charts for 84 weeks and peaked at number 2 (Billboard). His next album, *The Marshall Mathers LP*, included his song "Kill You," in which Eminem asks, "Slut, you think I won't choke no whore / 'til the vocal cords don't work in her throat no more?" (11-12). This only begins to show how graphic rappers are willing to go. In the same song, Eminem rants, "I invented violence, you vile venomous volatile bitches / vain Vicodin, vrinnn Vrinnn, VRINNN! [chainsaw sounds] / Texas Chainsaw, left his brains all danglin' from his neck, while his head barely hangs on" (23-26). Even with these lyrics, this album won the Best Rap Album award at the 2000 Grammy Awards (Grammy). These examples clearly show how popular violent rap is.

Some rappers say that these lyrics are not meant to be indicative of reality, and that they are pure fiction. Critics of hip-hop, however, suggest that violent lyrics like these, in the words of politician David Cameron, "[encourage] people to carry guns and knives" (qtd. in Rose 41). In her book *The Hip Hop Wars*, Tricia Rose argues that neither side's argument is completely valid. The quality of urban black life led to the introduction of violent themes as a way to express what the lower classes were feeling and hopefully to incite change. The urban African-American community, which was the inspiration for the early violent lyrics, had been slowly dying for several reasons: joblessness, increase in availability of weapons, loss of housing, the rise of illegal drugs, and the police's response in the form of "incarceration over rehabilitation" (Rose 48). Rappers sang about their lives at home and draw attention to the problems there. In the end, however, profits rose while the problems in the ghettos continued, and gangsta rappers still try to put forth the idea of change occurring through their music as a justification for their repulsive lyrics.

Misogyny is another problem in the current rap scene. There can be no question of the existence of misogyny in hip-hop music, and it is not the fault entirely of the corporations or of the artists. Rather it is a burden shared by both. Rappers like Lil Wayne, Nelly, Jay-Z and Snoop Dogg constantly insult and demean women (especially black women). The group N.W.A also helped start this trend. One of their members, M.C. Ren, explains his relationship with women in this way: "Women? Oh, man, I love women, man! I don't like bitches.

Bitches like motherfuckers just for they money. . . . Everybody in my group love [sic] women; we just hate bitches" (qtd. in Rhym). This statement assumes that these rappers have the right to label certain women and sort them into categories (Rhym). The main lyricist of N.W.A, Ice Cube, stated that he believed rappers should act as role models, but in his song, "I Ain't the 1," he states:

> See they think we narrow-minded
> Cause they got a cute face, and big-behinded
> So I walk over and say "How ya doin?"
> See I'm only down for screwin, but you know
> Ya gotta play it off cool
>
> . . . .
>
> Run out of money, and watch your heart break
> They'll drop you like a bad habit
> Cause a brother with money yo, they gotta have it.
> (9-13, 20-22)

Ice Cube simultaneously brags about fooling women and lying about his intentions toward them, and complains that when his money disappears, the women do as well.

Other major rappers often show their disdain for women. Aside from the aforementioned "Tip Drill," Nelly has several songs that show his lack of respect for women. One of these is the song "Pimp Juice," in which Nelly remarks, "I lay the ladies (ooh) like they should get laid" (36) in one verse, and in another says "One-touch sunroof ("BOOP!") leave it alone / Hoes see it, can't believe it - "It's goin' back on its own" (12-13). Obviously Nelly believes that he is superior.

Unfortunately, men dominate the rap industry. Rarely do female artists appear on a hit rap song, and finding a female rapper herself is ever rarer. Many of these female artists, like Lauryn Hill and Sarah Jones, seek to empower women with their words. One example is "Your Revolution" by Sarah Jones, in which Jones uses explicit language in reverse, " Your revolution will not be you smacking it up, flipping it, or rubbing it down. / Nor will it take you downtown or humping around. / Because that revolution will not happen between these thighs" (qtd. in Rose 123).

On the other hand, sometimes explicit language used by black women rappers isn't so empowering. Many of them, such as Lil' Kim and Foxy Brown use the same language as male misogynist rappers do, under a veil of breaking through sexist barriers. In her 2003 duet with 50 Cent, "Magic Stick," Lil' Kim states that she can "sex a nigga so good, he gotta tell his boys" (32). Lil' Kim uses the same language as the male rappers who dominate the industry use, despite the fact that a female is supposedly in control during these songs (qtd. in Rose 124). Critic Tricia Rose argues that in this way, the rap industry betrays the women of color who listen to its music.

Rose describes the two different kinds of people who attack hip-hop's misogyny: a) the people who use it to denigrate hip-hop as a whole, and b) the progressively-minded people who want to elevate women's rights and image. Most of the outrage against hip-hop because of its anti-woman aspect ignores the effect this music actually has on the image of black women and instead focuses on the problems with the genre entirely. Another problem is the marrying of the issues of sexually degrading language (words like "bitch" and "ho") and sexually explicit language. Rose argues that if the idea of any explicit language becomes "filthy" is the eyes of society, then "women's own sexual freedom and autonomy is at stake" (123). Women won't be allowed to use explicit language to empower each other if all explicit language is frowned upon. Tricia Rose believes that to challenge the rampant sexism in hip-hop, society must have three goals; to attack the sexism in hip-hop for the right reasons and not for anti-black or religious causes; to support hip-hop's up and coming artists who do not support the current anti-female culture; and to educate the youth of America about sexism, what it means and how we can fight it (131).

Fortunately, there is a sizable movement away from misogynistic themes in the music by artists who are currently rising in the hip-hop music scene. Lupe Fiasco, whose most recent album *Lupe Fiasco's The Cool* debuted at number fifteen on the Billboard 200 and went gold, focuses on political and social themes such as the war in Iraq, growing up without a father, and living around drugs. Kid Cudi, whose debut album *Man on the Moon: The End of Day* was released in September 2009, often focuses on love and human emotion in his songs, rarely showing disrespect towards women and never advocating violence. Of course, some veteran rappers have been able to stray from violence and misogyny for their whole careers. Common, whose career began in 1992, is one of the few artists who can be regarded as "clean" in terms of content. His lyrics focus on love and social problems, and he completely eschews gangsterism. The hip-hop artists Talib Kweli and Mos Def, who together make up the group Black Star, are yet another example. Their debut album, *Mos Def & Talib Kweli are Black Star*, is about philosophical ideas and modern-day issues. Their song "Brown-Skin Lady" is a tribute to brown-skinned women, and the lyrics tell them to be proud of their hair and complexion and not to be influenced by Western beauty standards. Kweli rhymes:

> We're not dealin' with the European standard of
> beauty tonight
> Turn off the TV and put the magazine away
> In the mirror tell me what you see
> See the evidence of divine presence (107-110)

Rap and hip-hop artists must realize how much influence and sway they hold over the youth of this country. In his review of the movie *Dangerous Minds* in 1995, Roger Ebert remarked:

> Rap has a bad reputation in white circles, where many
> people believe it consists of obscene and violent anti-
> white and anti-female guttural. Some of it does. Most
> does not. . . .[R]ap plays the same role today as Bob
> Dylan did in 1960, giving voice to the hopes and
> angers of a generation, and a lot of rap is powerful
> writing.

This quote exemplifies the power that rap wields.

Some rappers use their power to influence young people towards equality and love, while others utilize rap only to make money. Even though the most popular rappers today are almost all the latter, there is still hope. Most young rappers are moving in a different direction in terms of theme. Although rappers like Jay-Z, Lil Wayne, and 50 Cent still dominate the charts, newer trends seem to be slowly sweeping them to the side. Increasingly, they are sharing the spotlight with artists like Kid Cudi or Lupe Fiasco, and in the future, perhaps our society will spend its time listening to an evolved form of hip-hop, one that shares the spotlight between the sexes and draws attention to ghetto life without promoting it.

Works Cited

"Billboard 200: Week of March 13th, 1999." *Billboard.com*. 2009. Web. 23 Nov 2009.

Black Star. "Brown Skin Lady." *Mos Def & Talib Kweli are Black Star*. Rawkus/Priority/EMI Records, 1998. CD.

Chang, Jeff. *Can't Stop Won't Stop: A History of the Hip-Hop Generation*. New York, NY: St. Martin's Press, 2005. Print.

Ebert, Roger. "Dangerous Minds." *Rogerebert.com*. 11 Aug 1995. Web. 23 Nov 2009.

Eminem. "Kill You." *The Slim Shady LP*. Aftermath/Interscope, 1999. CD.

Eminem. *The Slim Shady LP*. Aftermath/Interscope, 1999. CD.

"Grammy Award Winners." *Grammy.com*. 2009. The Recording Academy, Web. 23 Nov 2009.

Nelly. "Pimp Juice." *Nellyville*. Universal Records/Fo' Reel Entertainment, 2002. CD.

Nelly. "Tip Drill." *Country Grammar*. Universal Motown, 2000. MP3.

N.W.A. "Fuck tha Police." *Straight Outta Compton*. Priority/Ruthless, 1988. CD.

N.W.A. "I Ain't the One." *Straight Outta Compton*. Performed by Ice Cube. Priority/Ruthless, 1988. CD.

Rhym, Darren. "'Here's for the Bitches': An Analysis of Gangsta Rap and Misogyny." *Womanist Theory and Research*. (1996) Web. 23 Nov 2009.

Rose, Tricia. "Hip Hop Demeans Women." *The Hip Hop Wars: What We Talk About When We Talk About Hip Hop and Why It Matters*. USA: Basic Civitas Books, 2008. 113-131. Print.

Rose, Tricia. "Hip Hop Causes Violence" *The Hip Hop Wars: What We Talk About When We Talk About Hip Hop and Why It Matters*. USA: Basic Civitas Books, 2008. 33-60. Print.

Living With His Tears
JOSEPH NUSSBAUM

Music is a form of art that touches and moves the soul; we derive feelings from music. Music gives all the opportunity to express ourselves freely; we associate our lives to songs that we listen to or sing. Music is "the science or art of ordering tones or sounds in succession, in combination, and in temporal relationships to produce a composition having unity and continuity" (*Merriam-Webster*). We develop connections between songs and our lives and, thus, take ownership of these songs. Songs can be funny, beautiful, joyful, festive, or sad. Unfortunately, Eric Clapton's "Tears in Heaven" is a very moving song that reaches out and touches our souls. Eric Clapton pours his soul out in this song; we feel the pain in his voice, in his lyrics, in his instruments. The theme of Eric Clapton's somber song "Tears in Heaven" presents us with the issue of life after death. Clapton apologizes for the loss of his son who he will need to guide him through his life and who he will rely on to be there for him in heaven.

Clapton wrote "Tears in Heaven" when he was going through a terrible time in his life. This song medicated Clapton's heart and soul after "his 4-year-old son, Conor, died when he fell out of a 53rd floor window in the apartment where his mother was staying in New York City" ("Tears"). Clapton puts his heartbreaking experience of losing his son in a song; he wonders if he will ever see him again. The death pushed Clapton "into depression. From it emerged "Tears in Heaven," Clapton's most successful song" (Woloschuk 1). In fact, "[Tears in Heaven] won Grammys in 1993 for Record of the Year, Song of the Year, [and] Clapton was nominated for nine Grammys that year and won six" ("Tears").

When he wrote this song, his life was in shambles. Clapton was hurting during the production of "Tears in Heaven"; this song touches everyone who has lost someone important in their lives. Clapton states that "Tears in Heaven" was "never meant for publication or public consumption"; it was just what he did to stop from going mad (Clapton 250). This song holds a great meaning and purpose for all those who listen to and cherish this piece.

"Tears in Heaven" is composed in such a sorrowful melody that, in terms of tone, it contributes to the song's theme. Clapton wrote this as an apologetic ballad to ask forgiveness for not being present when his son fell to his death. While listening to the song, we hear Clapton sing with remorse and regret, as if he was talking directly to his son. He asks questions to Conor throughout the song, adding more sorrow because he is acting as if he still had the ability to communicate with him. The sorrowful tone and melody of the song may be classified as an elegy. The music is slow-paced and soft-sung which causes listeners to feel Clapton's words of mourning. The instruments used in the song are two acoustic guitars and a piano accompanying Clapton's mournful voice. That the song is played with acoustic instruments tells the listeners that this is untouched by production; it adds a personal feeling to the song. The sorrowful and apologetic tone reaffirms that Clapton is in mourning.

The lyrics of "Tears in Heaven" are so short and precise, yet of great importance that they help explain the theme of the song. This song is, by far, Clapton's greatest and most powerful song because each line flows harmoniously which adds a deeper meaning to the song. Clapton states, "I must be strong / And carry on," which implies that he is weak but understands that he does not belong with Conor (5, 6). In fact, there is a role reversal between father and son when Clapton asks, "Would you hold my hand / If I saw you in Heaven?" and "Would you help me stand / If I saw you in heaven?" (9, 10, 11, 12) Clapton is asking his son for help and guidance through the terrible situation that he is experiencing. Clapton is sorry for the death of his son and blames himself because of it. He wants Conor to forgive him and, hopefully, one day they will meet and reunite in heaven.

Clapton asks questions directly of Conor. Clapton's ballad asks his son "would you know my name / if I saw you in heaven?" (1, 2) Clapton wants to know if Conor will be willing to see him again, in heaven. "Would it be the same / if I saw you in heaven?" asks Clapton—or will you blame me for your death? (3) Clapton realizes that Conor is in heaven and knows that he cannot bring him back; "[he knows he does not] belong here in heaven" (7). These questions within the song show us that Clapton is searching for answers. This song speaks to everyone and anyone who has ever lost someone close to them. Clapton's questioning and speculating of whether his son will forgive him and guide him through life adds tremendous meaning to the theme.

Songs, such as Clapton's "Tears in Heaven," make us feel sorry and mournful for those we have lost. He speaks to listeners and helps them cope with their troubles. In the song, he reveals a deeper message of how precious life is. Life can be easily taken away in the blink of an eye. Clapton experienced "a tragic sense of loss" and wrote the song in that state of mind. This sense of loss "has shaped Eric Clapton's music more than anything else" (Woloschuk 3). Clapton says, "I wrote this one to ask the question I had been asking myself ever since my grandfather had died. Will we really ever meet again? It's difficult to talk about these songs in depth, that's why they're songs" (Clapton 251). "Tears in Heaven," presents us with the issue of life after death; once somebody close to us dies, will we ever meet that person again?

Works Cited

Clapton, Eric. "Tears in Heaven." *Rush Soundtrack*, 1999. CD.

Clapton, Eric. *Clapton: The Autobiography*. New York: Broadway Books, 2007. Print.

The Merriam-Webster Dictionary. Springfield, Massachusetts: Merriam-Webster, Incorporated, 2004. Print.

"Tears in Heaven by Eric Clapton." *Songfacts*. n. p. 2007. Web. 27 Oct 2008.

"Tears in Heaven by Eric Clapton and Will Jennings." *Eric Clapton Lyric Archive*. n. p. 2007. Web. 27 Oct 2008.

Woloschuk, Michael. "*Citizen* Writer Michael Woloschuk Discovers the Lost Father who Haunts Eric Clapton's Music." *The Ottawa Citizen* n.p., n.d. Web. 27 Oct 2008.

Seeing *Casablanca*: "Life in the Reel"
HOPE M. MAHON

Casablanca. This story continually moves me. When I gaze at the film's publicity poster, I find that it artfully reveals this story of two people caught in a turbulent world, exposes a unique time in history, and at the same time, recalls my Irish grandfather. In this illustration, I see themes of acute happiness, times of deep passion, realizations of profound truths, and circumstances of bottomless sorrow. It is "life in the reel."

My obsession with *Casablanca* stems from a lust for a period other than my own, a thirst for unresolved romance, and a passion for less-than-perfect endings. Within such settings lies truth, reality, not the evasion of reality. Life pains us, complicates, confuses and often possesses no resolutions as films normally offer us.

If the observer finds herself unfamiliar with the *Casablanca* chronicle, she need only gaze at this poster for insight. As clearly indicated by the manner in which the images are laid out, the film centers upon two individuals, Rick and Ilsa, who are at the center of the poster. Their love story unfolds amidst the onset of World War II culminating with an unlikely encounter in Casablanca, French Morocco.

When observing the *Casablanca* poster, one notices that the dark background calls to mind fireworks, or an explosive environment. The observer may wonder: Is the yellow light between Ilsa and Rick a sunrise, a sunset, or perhaps a detonating bomb? The spark-like frays surrounding Ilsa and Rick form abstract palm leaves. Whatever the interpretation, one discovers in the image the whispers of a crumbling and chaotic world of human helplessness.

Rick's costume illuminates the period of history when "night clubs" were fashionable and when everyone (who was anyone) smoked. Below the profiles of Rick and Ilsa emerges a water-washed image of a plane. This visual element further reveals the time period calling attention to the central role of "the plane" in the story *Casablanca*. On the right, buildings of a near ancient quality emerge from the backdrop, hinting to the film's location, but also pointing to the past. Even if she has not seen the film, the casual observer must conclude these objects play integral roles in the story.

Rick stands pictured again, as a small figure in the forefront. The iconic man known as "Rick" appears isolated, perhaps alienated. He is reminiscent of a lone ranger of the Wild West. Rick's portrayal in this instance personifies his sorrow, his eventual reconciliation to himself, to the world, and with truth. "Rick," played by Humphrey Bogart, connects me to my grandfather, who looked and sounded like him. Both were young and handsome during the 1950s; both were from the New York City crowd: a class of straight-talkers, joke-crackers, and serious smokers and drinkers. Both possess a raw self-assuredness, a charismatic demeanor, and a no bullshit attitude, unforgettable to a young girl.

When analyzing the central figures of Ilsa and Rick, the viewer is struck by the complexity in their expressions, revealing the complexity of their turbulent love affair. The lovers stare purposefully. In calm passion? In sad acceptance? In love's blissful denial? There is a subtle sadness pervading their stares. The careful observer will ask: "Why do they appear sad?" or "Why aren't they happily in love?" Rick and Ilsa's deep passion reveals a profound truth. The termination of Rick and Ilsa's liaison ultimately results in sorrow, yet concludes in hopeful expectation: a future beyond themselves and a war-laden world.

Why do I love this image? Why does this story never fail to arouse me? I love this image because it highlights life as it is—wildly happy, miserable, and sad. It also reminds me of someone whom I lost, who was at once challenging, unforgettable, and chaotic. I love what I regain when I watch this film. I love how the film draws the viewer in, holds her as a witness, as a hostage, forcing her question her own existence. This image reveals a passionate existence, while quietly alluding to a specific society in a specific moment in time. But the message this image conveys, though culturally dated, permeates into any time period and is universal.

What society will not face friction, hardship, or heartache? Such topics may be among the strongest common threads individuals share. Who is not moved by or cannot relate with such themes? We love, we feel pain, while a crazy world surrounds us. This is reality. This is *Casablanca*.

Work Cited

Casablanca. Dir. Michael Curtiz. Perf. Humphrey Bogart, Ingrid Bergman. Warner Brothers, 1942. Film.

Martín Espada and the Revolution
Against Cultural Assimilation
SAM BORENZWEIG

"Let us waste no time in sterile litanies and nauseating mimicry," states Frantz Fanon, condemning Europe's shadow over Africa. Fanon gets his people to reject European principles in The Wretched of the Earth, a revolutionary text calling for the Algerian people to move towards decolonization. Although Africa is no longer lawfully chained by European imperialism, cultural assimilation maintains the West's grasp on the continent.

Just as the former European colonies of Africa unconsciously have clung to the ways of their colonizers, many Puerto Ricans idealize American culture and have assimilated accordingly. Martín Espada ruminates on the consequence' of cultural assimilation in his poem, "Coca Cola and Coco Frío," published in his 1993 collection *City of Coughing and Dead Radiators*. The poem tells of a boy from Brooklyn who travels to Puerto Rico for the first time to visit his relatives. He does not immerse himself in his native culture by speaking Spanish and eating Puerto Rican delicacies. Rather, his family bombards him with fragmented English, American jingles from television, and Coca-Cola.

Martín Espada was born in Brooklyn, New York in 1957 to a Puerto Rican father and a Jewish mother ("Martín Espada"). Espada was greatly influenced by the struggles of his immigrant father, and many of his poems focus on the hardships that Latin newcomers face in the United States ("Martín Espada"). Espada's poetry, at times tinged with the bite of an angry revolutionary, has been the subject of controversy, even in the most progressive forums. In 1997, National Public Radio rescinded an invitation to Espada to read a poem on air for National Poetry Month, when he selected a poem about the controversial imprisonment of Mumia Abu-Jamal ("The NPR Censorship of Martín Espada").

In "Coca-Cola and Coco Frío," Espada returns to his activist roots and criticizes the United States' imperialist relationship with the all-too-eager-to-please Puerto Rico. In *The Wretched of the Earth*, Frantz Fanon also exposes the United States as an imperialist force: "Two centuries ago, a former European colony decided to catch up with Europe. It succeeded so well that the United State of America became a monster, in which the taints, the sickness and the inhumanity of Europe have grown to appalling dimensions" (Fanon). One of the "colonies" that the United States possesses is Puerto Rico, which is a commonwealth and territory. Despite and possibly because of its close ties with the United States, most of Puerto Rico is desperately impoverished ("Welcome to Puerto Rico!"). The little wealth that the island holds comes from Americans and other Westerners who, lounging behind the gates of the Ritz Carlton, are able to shield themselves from substandard living conditions and destitution.

In "Coca-Cola and Coco Frío," the boy from Brooklyn personifies the United States: "the fat boy wandered / from table to table / with his mouth open" (lines 3-5). This depicts a stereotypical mentality; Espada characterizes the United States as greedy, with a childish sense of entitlement. The choice of the verb "wander" implies ignorance and naïveté. The boy does not know what he wants, so he aimlessly tastes everything. However, he is satisfied with nothing, for it is merely a regurgitation of what he has experienced back home: "he was bored with this potion, familiar / from soda fountains in Brooklyn" (12-13). This "potion" is Coca-Cola.

The word "potion" conveys a sense of witchcraft and evil. Coca-Cola wields a mysterious power over the people of Puerto Rico. It is a symbol of globalization and a new era of imperialism, one no better than that of the European colonizers in Africa in 1961, when Fanon wrote *The Wretched of the Earth*. Coca Cola represents not only the commercial culture of the United States, but also the immense impact that American corporations have upon the world. The Coca-Cola Company is the world's largest beverage company, manufacturer, distributor, and marketer, selling products in over 200 countries ("The Coca-Cola Company"). Over 40% of the Coca-Cola Company's revenue comes from Central and Latin America, and the world's second largest bottler, Coca-Cola FEMSA, is located in Mexico ("The Coca-Cola Company"). The Coca-Cola Company has long been the subject of criticism in the hum rights arena, and the corporation has settled dozens of lawsuits regarding discrimination and other unethical practices such as violently repressing unions at bottling plants in South America ("The Coca-Cola Company"). It has been criticized as a fascist monopoly, valuing profitability far above preserving the rights and dignity of people in the third world. Globalization and American corporations such as the Coca-Cola Company are at fault for the cultural assimilation that is slowly eroding the Puerto Rican way of life.

The boy's relatives, who personify Puerto Rico, "steer him" to the beverage "with cool spotted hands . . . One even sang to him, in all the English / she could remember, a Coca-Cola jingle / from the forties" (7-11). They seek to impress the boy by being as American as possible. In this way, Espada portrays Puerto Ricans as naïve and passive as they strive to mimic the culture of their colonizers. These efforts are in vain, for Puerto Rico will never be exactly like the United States. It seems Espada is channeling Frantz Fanon, who asked, "How is it that we do not understand that we have better things to do than to follow that same Europe?" While the United States may be appealing to Puerto Ricans because of its wealth and power, Espada shows that Puerto Rico has treasures far more valuable: its history, heritage, and native culture.

Coco Frío, "a coconut / chilled, then scalped by a machete / so that a straw could inhale the clear milk," represents Puerto Rican culture (15- 7). The fresh, natural beverage, which translates to "cold coconut," presents a strong juxtaposition against Coca-Cola, an artificial substance with an infinite shelf life. Coco Frío represents the forgotten natural beauty that is Puerto Rican culture:

> The boy tilted the green shell overhead
> and drooled coconut milk down his chin;
> suddenly, Puerto Rico was not Coca-Cola
> or Brooklyn, and neither was he. (18-21)

The boy is magically transported to a time before Puerto Rico drowned in the vapid, consumerist ways of America. He immediately feels connected with his roots, somewhere unlike "Coca-Cola / or Brooklyn" (20-21). The boy immerses himself fully in the grace of his unique and powerful heritage. This spiritual awakening provokes the boy's nostalgia for years afterward, but he is left questioning an island where

> ... the people drank Coca-Cola
> and sang jingles from World War II
> in a language they did not speak
> while so many coconuts in the trees
> sagged heavy and unsuckled. (22-28)

In comparing the unconsumed coconuts to a mother's breast, Espada shows that the Puerto Rican people are refusing their own culture and resources like a baby who refuses to feed. This will most certainly lead to the death of the baby; likewise, the Puerto Rican culture will become so malnourished that it will eventually disappear altogether. Espada channels Frantz Fanon once again, calling for the Puerto Rican people to liberate themselves from their futile quest to live up to Western ideals.

Frantz Fanon states, "Moreover, if we wish to reply to the expectations of the people of Europe, it is no good sending them back a reflect on, even an ideal reflection, their society and their thought with which from time to time they feel immeasurably sickened" (Fanon). The glimmer of hope that resonates in this poem comes from the boy, who is disenchanted (not quite "immeasurably sickened") with American culture, then enamored with the untapped potential of his native people and culture. Although Espada selects Puerto Rico as the subject of "Coca-Cola and Coco Frío," he is calling for a resistance to complete cultural assimilation throughout the world. Frantz Fanon calls to his people, asking them to "turn over a new leaf . . . work out new concepts, and try to set afoot a new man" (Fanon). But who is this "new man?" It is a new age of humanity in which people need not conform to a dominant culture, but rather celebrate the uniqueness and individuality of their own way of life.

Works Cited

Espada, Martín. "Coca-Cola & Coco Frio." *City of Coughing and Dead Radiators.* New York: W. W. Norton & Company, Inc., 1993. 26-27. Print.

Fanon, Frantz. *The Wretched of the Earth.* 1st edition. New York, NY: Grove Press, 2004. Print.

"Espada, Martín." *Martín Espada: Poet, Essayist, Editor & Translator.* Web. 20 Apr 2009.

"Puerto Rico Economy." Welcome to Puerto Rico. 20 Apr 2009. Web.

"The Coca-Cola Company." Web.

Scotland: A Land Betrayed

ALYSSA FANE

Scottish poet, Edwin Muir, was undoubtedly unsettled with Scotland's condition during the first few decades of the twentieth century. His fears of human nature and opinions on the Scottish condition were central themes in much of his writing. His poem "The Town Betrayed" demonstrates how his background influenced his views on war and poverty in Scotland and how those views dictated the direction of his work from 1921-1951.

Edwin Muir was born in 1887 on a farm in the Orkneys, where he lived in a non-competitive farming community. The early part of his childhood was a time ". . . of unity, of timelessness, [and] of splendor," but the many hardships he faced as a young adult destroyed his youthful optimism (Butter 4). When Muir was fourteen his life changed drastically; his family moved from a small, traditional, agricultural community to Glasgow, a competitive industrial city that housed some of the "worst slums in Europe" (Butter 6). According to author P. H. Butter, although Muir was never destitute as those in Glasgow, he wrote in a personal letter that "the slums seemed to be everywhere around [him], a great, spreading swamp into which [he] might sink for good" (Butter 7). The economic regression that surrounded Muir stimulated his interest in Guild Socialism, a movement towards worker control in industry. During his teenage years, he experienced the death of his father and two brothers. Muir was emotionally troubled for a time, so he underwent psychoanalysis, which conjured many past emotions and memories that he had suppressed subconsciously. During Muir's twenties, he joined "The Intellectuals," a group that read and discussed the new literature and intellectual ideas of his time (Butter 9). This made him more observant of social injustice, and influenced his opinions about Guild Socialism and Nietzscheism, named for the German philosopher Nietzsche, who rejected Christian values and encouraged individuals to create their own moral principles (Butter 10). Muir began writing poetry when he was thirty-five years old. In his poetry, he acknowledged some the feelings and memories he'd uncovered during his psychoanalysis, as well as his opinions on the state of his homeland.

During Muir's lifetime, Scotland, as well as much of the world, was in an economic recession. Between the world wars, when Muir did most of his writing, Scotland experienced severe economic depression because its industrial economy focused on producing war materials. Unemployment, ill health, and poor living conditions became the norm there during the 1930s, particularly in Glasgow, where Muir spent much of his adolescence. The city was poor and dangerous; much of the population lived in slums and the sectarianism between Scottish Protestants and Irish Catholics caused hostility between the two groups over issues such as job competition, which led to gang formation and increased violence (BBC).

Muir's experiences molded him into a socially conscious individual and, according to Butter, the poet found it ". . . unbearable sometimes to look on and do nothing" (Butter 14). His poem, "The Town Betrayed" consists of ten quatrains, and draws from his personal experiences to demonstrate the sad state of his nation. Literary devices in "The Town Betrayed," such as repetition, rhyme, and alliteration enhance the artful presentation of his ideas.

Repetition of certain words throughout "The Town Betrayed" creates a feeling of unity among the poverty-stricken Scots. The speaker claims that

> Our homes are eaten out by time,
> Our lawns strewn with our listless sons,
> Our harlot daughters lean and watch
> The ships crammed down with shells and guns. (1-4)

The word "our" appears four times within the first stanza. The repetition is effective in incorporating Muir's intended audience into the poem, as a call to action. Rather than employing the first-person singular pronoun "I," which might evoke self-pity, the speaker includes all Scots. The tone of this stanza is sorrowful. By addressing all Scottish people, Muir applies the sadness in this portion of the poem. Words such as "our" or "we" throughout the poem increase its affect as a social protest piece because it implies that all of Scotland shares the grief for "listless sons," who have died in war (2).

Muir's childhood experiences made some of Scotland's social problems easily visible to him. His drastic move from the "non-competitive" farming community to the industrial monster of Glasgow, where he spent the last of his adolescent years, made clear to him the evils of the war-promoting industry. The line: "The ships crammed down with shells and guns" (4) acknowledges the relationship between Scotland's industry and the first two world wars. Muir had moved from a rural area to an urban area; likewise, he moved from peace to war. Muir's experiences gave him insight into political issues and social issues, which others may have perceived as commonplace. Someone who is accustomed to working in the city may not question the ethics of the industry there in the same way that one would if he or she had experienced life in an alternative environment.

The rhyme scheme in "The Town Betrayed" creates auditory unity throughout the poem. The last words in the second and fourth lines of each stanza rhyme. For example, in the third stanza the speaker states:

> Our yellow harvests lie forlorn
> And there we wander like the blind,
> Returning from the golden field
> With famine in our mind. (9-12)

The combination of the quatrain structure and masculine end rhyme make "The Town Betrayed" enjoyable to read, as it creates a singsong effect. Three of the four lines in this stanza end with the letter "d," which enhances the musicality of the piece by incorporating like sounds between the rhymes. However, the "d" sound in "blind" has a dark tone, and the sound repeats in the word "wander," as the people move without any sight or direction from the "field" (10-11).

The speaker addresses the poverty that Scottish population endured during the first third of the twentieth century in the following lines: "Returning from the golden field / With famine in our mind" (11-12). This refers to the hard working Scottish laborers who were not able to improve their own economic situation. Although unemployment rates were high between the world wars, people did work, yet remained poor. The government and its military benefited from the weapons and machinery produced by workers, who rarely increased their personal economic growth. Thus, they lived in some of "the worst slums in Europe" (Butter 6).

Alliteration, a series of like sounds, draws attention to certain details in the poem, especially in the sixth stanza:

> We stand beside our windows, see
> In order dark disorder come,
> And prentice killers duped by death
> Bring and not know our doom. (21-24)

The repetition of the "d" and "o" sounds in this particular stanza enhance the musical quality of the rhythmic pattern that is already in place in the rest of the poem; the initial alliteration makes this stanza stand out among the rest. This section of "The Town Betrayed" conveys the harshest consequence of war and poverty: death. Death looms constantly ". . . beside [their] windows . . ." (21). Whether the Scots were starving to death, or fighting in war or in the streets, it was difficult to survive, let alone to prosper.

Muir experienced the death of his father and two brothers when he was young; thus, death was an inescapable end that he understood too well. Moreover, he witnessed the unnecessary death and suffering of those in Glasgow. He had lost his closest family members to illness, but there were people all over Scotland dying unnecessarily due to war, gang fare, disease, and starvation. If only Scotland would have improved its economy by directing its industry to produce something other than war materials or by possibly creating a welfare system, many of these deaths could have been prevented.

Muir's background influenced his beliefs about the world beyond his town, inspiring him to produce social protest poetry. The shift from an agricultural to an industrial community formed his critical views on capitalism; he saw the poor struggle in the city streets and decided, with the help of the political groups like "The Intellectuals," that their level of poverty was unacceptable. His support of workers' rights and Guild Socialism are effects of the poverty he witnessed. The death of much of Muir's family revealed to him the consequences of warfare. Death was a likely occurrence at this time, which troubled Muir deeply. He'd observed that war causes death in battle, as well as hardships for the workers at home making the tools and weapons for the soldiers on the front line. Wars, abroad and in Glasgow, seemed endless, which caused a state of hopelessness in the Scots that Muir represented in the first stanza of "The Town Betrayed."

"The Town Betrayed" is a poem of social protest against the war and industrialism. The industry-based economy in Scotland sustained war and caused fighting on the home front due to job competition among religious groups. The break between the two world wars left many people without work, which led to even more severe poverty; no matter the state of war in Scotland, it people were suffering. Toward the end of the poem, the speaker asserts, "Watching as if his tents were time / And Troy eternity" (35-36). According to critic Roger Knight, Muir alludes to Troy to signify the presence of "wars and betrayals, past and future. . . . With no loss of distinction between ancient and modern practice" (Knight 74). The themes of wars and of betrayal are timeless; although one would think that humanity would learn from the mistakes of the past, Muir points out that humans have continued to engage in warfare since ancient times. He wants his people to observe the consequences of war so that they might change. In "The Town Betrayed," Muir addresses the troubles in Scotland as those of the whole nation. Through the first-person plural point of view, the speaker involves all citizens in his discussion of the poor Scottish condition, encouraging a shared sense of responsibility. As a concerned Scot, Muir reveals the common Scot's suffering to persuade his people that such problems are their own. He does so as a call to action.

The protest poem "The Town Betrayed" is important both as a plea for change and as a historical account of early twentieth century Scotland. During Muir's lifetime, his poetry served to spread awareness and stimulate reactions from the common Scottish citizen, in hope that their corresponding actions may improve the quality of life for all people. If read historically, the poem represents the socioeconomic and cultural conditions in Scotland during the 1900s from the perspective of an educated person who lived through it. This poem is more than a work of art; it remains a sober warning to new generations and people of all cultures about the damage of war, including class struggle and inter-community violence.

Works Cited

Butter, P. H. *Edwin Muir*. Edinburgh: Oliver and Boyd Ltd, 1962. Print.

Knight, Roger. *Edwin Muir: An Introduction to His Work*. New York: Longman Inc., 1980. Print.

Muir, Edwin. *Collected Poems*. New York: Oxford University Press, 1960. Print.

"20th Century Scotland -An Introduction (II)." BBC. Web. 23 Mar 2009.

The Argumentative Essay

In an argumentative essay, the author makes a claim and supports it through the use of evidence. While the primary purpose of an argumentative essay is to convince the reader of the validity of the author's position, another purpose may be to encourage the reader to take a particular action. Examples of argumentative writing include editorials, letters to the editor, and opinion pieces.

The Unseen Value of Immigrants
FRANCIS RODRIGUEZ

She could hear the commotion surrounding her as she closed her eyes, lying in the delivery room for the second time in her life. As she lay there in pain, she fell into an occurrence of déjà vu. She was giving life to another baby, except this time around, it was a girl, a dream come true. But something was missing. She opened her eyes, hoping she could see her husband standing next to her experiencing this beautiful event with her. She knew it was a foolish wish. The pain was overwhelming her, but she realized it wasn't physical pain that took over her body. It was coming from a deeper, more internal and personal place. Her mother was there with her, but it did not fill the empty space she felt in her chest. The sorrow she felt overshadowed the pain and joy of having another baby. Deep down she knew the hard path that lay ahead for her children. She had faced the same harsh fate with her siblings. Growing up fatherless was going to haunt her children the same way it had haunted her. In the eyes of the United States government, the fact that her husband was an illegal immigrant negated all the positive qualities he possessed. Although he was a hardworking and devoted husband and father, he had been deported. This is the tragic and inspirational story of a single mother, Belkys Cruz.

This story is merely a small glimpse into the millions of stories that are being experienced nationwide. The life of an immigrant is not an easy one. Not only do they take on the worst jobs in order to place food on their families' tables, but they also have to worry constantly that the United States government will put an end to their opportunities. The government underestimates the value of every immigrant in the country. Immigrants are an essential factor in the stimulation of the economy. While it is true that being an immigrant without going through the proper government channels is illegal, the guidelines for prosecuting these immigrants should be revised so that the immigrant's work, family, background, and history are considered before deciding to deport him or her.

Immigration is a controversial topic, and the residents of the United States are divided when it comes to the action that should be taken in regards to illegal immigration. Opponents of illegal immigration argue that immigrants impact job availability, health care, national security and border control. They argue that immigrants are willing to take unattractive, low-wage jobs away from citizens. However, we depend on these illegal immigrants to fill 90 percent of the agricultural occupations, jobs legal residents/citizens won't do. Many people also argue that illegal immigrants cost the government millions of dollars in regards to healthcare. Whether they have insurance or not, these men, women and children must be given medical attention in emergency rooms. However, the majority of the immigrant population is actually scared of signing up for public assistance such as Medicaid because they fear that they might leave a paper trail leading to being apprehended. Another argument against illegal immigrants is based on the money spent on border control. The truth of the matter is that no matter what the government does to control the border there are still agents letting immigrants in the country because they know the immigrants will reward them with money. Many of these points are arguable, but they are also filled with half-truths and fallacies. One problem with many people who call for the deportation of illegal immigrants is that they often view them as a group of lawbreakers instead of as individuals.

Every year illegal immigrants pay taxes with the persistent dream of one day being able to be legal, and the American government benefits from their desire. When these immigrants give their employers fake social security numbers, they are then required to pay taxes. Unfortunately, the money that they are paying in taxes cannot be claimed upon retirement because they cannot file income taxes. The government received an astonishing $189 billion from "unknown sources" of Social Security earnings during the 1990s. After years of investigating, Social Security realized that this huge influx of money into the economy was a direct result of immigration. Government officials are very much aware of who is hiring these illegal immigrants and exploiting their cheap labor, but they do little to stop or punish them. Apparently, the advantage of having an extra $189 billion to stimulate the American economy is much more important than having trespassers on our land. In the current decade, this revenue stream is growing, on average, by more than $50 billion a year, generating $6 billion to $7 billion in Social Security tax revenue and about $1.5 billion in Medicare taxes every year (White). Especially in times of recession, our country needs any type of stimulus to the economy it can get; therefore keeping the immigrants is an economic positive.

Despite the fact that immigrants work under some of the most difficult conditions, such as in meatpacking and agriculture, their readiness to do this work does not receive any consideration when it comes to their deportation. "Without the help of immigrant labor, the US economy would virtually collapse. We want and need cheap immigrant labor, but we do not want the immigrants" (White). Employers love having workers who are paid virtually nothing. Many Americans complain that the immigrants take their jobs, but if employers were to lose their immigrant workers, they would likely end up investing in new technology rather than paying higher wages to citizens; ultimately replacing workers with automation (Davidson). The American consumer also benefits from the low wages being paid to immigrants as low wages mean that companies pay less to produce their goods; therefore, we pay less. Americans are blind when it comes to seeing that these immigrants are the backbone of our economy. The least they could have is some consideration when it comes to being penalized by the government for their immigration status.

Like many other Americans, immigrants are involved in criminal acts. For example, when a person trespasses without the permission of the property owner it is considered a criminal act. But when these trespassers are a large part of the country's economy, there should be some type of consideration given to them. It is true, as many critics point out, that some immigrants, instead of taking advantage of America's opportunities, vandalize property and commit other crimes. Yes, these are the immigrants should be prosecuted and deported. However, the government should not penalize those immigrants who struggle and sacrifice every day to make a living in this nation.

American citizens should realize the full consequences of deportation. Most families that lose a parent to deportation eventually experience a finical crisis. Often the person being deported has children who depend on them. The children are the ones that suffer the most in these cases. Growing up with only one parent, these children have a disadvantage, perhaps leading them, eventually, to commit crimes. After deportation, these families carry and indescribable burden of stress and poverty.

As Belkys Cruz holds the phone, all she can do is cry. Hundreds of happy memories flow into her head as she speaks to him. She reminisces about the long nights when she had her husband on one side and her son on the other, memories of when she used to be the happiest women in the world. He tries to talk to her, but the words don't seem to register in Belkys's head. Eventually she hangs up because she can't bear the sound of his voice and the pain she feels. As she lies down on her bed, she looks in her children's eyes and sees that they too feel pain, but it is not quite like hers. They are too young to realize what has happened. The pain is a pain that could have been avoided if their father had been given a chance to prove that he was more than an "illegal immigrant." Once again, the hope of a family has been destroyed.

Works Cited

"Comprehensive Reform of Our Immigration Laws." *National Immigration Forum*. n. p. Sept. 2008. Web. 21 Nov. 2008.

Davidson, Adam. "Q&A: Illegal Immigrants and the U.S. Economy." *NPR.org*, NPR, 30 Mar. 2006. Web. 2 Dec. 2008.

White, Deborah. "Why the Federal Government Can't End Illegal Immigration." *About.com*. n.d. Web. 2 Dec. 2008.

Animal Testing: An Immoral Practice
CAROLYN CANDELA

Imagine being forced to spend your life in a laboratory locked in a cage packed with other human beings. You do not know what you are doing there or whether you are safe. One day a man in a white lab coat lifts you out of the cage. You have no idea where you are being taken or what is going to happen. Unfortunately, this nightmare is a reality for millions of lab animals who are raised for testing purposes. For years, medical companies have been taking advantage of animals in order to experiment with new medications. Universities and schools have also experimented on animals for educational purposes. Until recently, there was relatively little debate in the general public over experimenting on animals. Now, as people discover new methods of experimentation, they are beginning to question the morality of testing on animals.

In many laboratories, the experiments that scientists perform on animals are terrifying. These experimental procedures include everything from injections and stomach tubes, to the implanting of electrodes into the animal's skin. In many cases, laboratory animals are given medications that allow them to reproduce unnatural amounts of offspring. This is done so that the scientists have more animals on which to test different products (Coalition). There is no doubt that some laboratory animals have similar anatomies to humans, which can be valuable in terms of determining the effects of a drug on human beings. However, this also means that, in many cases, animals are able to feel pain to the same extent that humans do. Many scientists have tried to develop procedures containing anesthetics so that less pain is inflicted upon the animals. Still, these animals are at a high risk for death. We must ask ourselves whether it is moral to take the life of an animal in order to save a human. Many people care for their pets and treat them as if they were family members; they believe that animals' lives have value, just as humans' lives do.

Over time, the life expectancy of the human race has increased due to the elimination of many lethal diseases, including smallpox and scarlet fever. Most people automatically assume that these improvements are solely due to testing vaccines and medication on animals. However, the elimination of these diseases from Western civilization is mostly due to improved standards of living and sanitation (Greek). This is not to say that animal research has not benefited humans. Indeed, many medical improvements have included some form of animal testing. Yet, animal-tested products have not always had the same effects on humans as they did on the tested animals. In fact, between the years of 1976 and 1985, 51.5 percent of 198 tested drugs caused reactions in humans serious enough to remove them from the market, altogether (Carlson). Cancers behave differently in animals than they do in humans as well, so cancer treatments tested on animals are often not effective on humans. Since animals and humans have similar anatomies, people often assume that animals are the best sources on which to test human medication. It makes sense that with similar anatomies, medication may react similarly in both species. Unfortunately, since illnesses react differently in different species of mammals, the results are never fully predictable.

Many people wonder what may happen if animal testing were ever prohibited. How would we know which medications are safe? Thankfully, progress is being made in finding alternate sources of experimentation. Certain types of alternative testing methods have proven to be just as effective, if not more effective, than testing on animals. One of these methods is the Human Skin Model, also known as the EpiDerm test. This procedure uses human skin left over from surgeries, as well as donated cadavers (Greek). Chemicals are applied to the skin to see how they penetrate and how dangerous they are to humans. This test successfully replaces the painful skin corrosion studies performed on rabbits. Scientists are continuing to make progress with finding alternate ways of experimentation, which do not include harming animals.

Only a small number of laboratories currently rely on alternate sources. In the meantime, people could take preventative measures that would save innocent animals. Scientists should continue to develop methods of experimentation that require fewer animals. If a minimal amount of animals were subject to such experiments, more animals would not have to endure ill-treatment. In addition, reducing the amount of lab animals (and eventually eliminating their need) would save money. Excess animals and equipment require funding. Instead of investing money in these animals and equipment, the government could fund alternate experiments with cell and tissue cultures (Pardue).

The ethics of animal experimentation is a controversial issue in classrooms across the country. In thousands of biology labs each year, students dissect animals in order to learn more about human and animal anatomy. These animals die solely to serve as models for studying anatomy and experimentation. Dissecting animals in schools sends the message to students that it is ethical to experiment on animals. Today, instead of harming actual animals in order to teach anatomy and physiology, students can access virtual dissections on the internet. This way, students can observe and understand anatomy while learning humaneness (Lewis).

Human beings have experimented on millions of animals for medical and educational purposes. Recently, scientists have discovered alternate methods of testing which do not require animals. These methods, including the use of human skin samples and cell cultures, have proven to be as effective in medicine as testing on animals. Although medications for many diseases have proven successful through animal experimentation, other medications that worked on animals in the testing phase were harmful to humans. It is very important that people become educated about alternate means of experimentation, and that in most cases, animal testing is unnecessary and immoral.

Works Cited

Carlson, Peggy. "Animal Medical Experimentation Is Unjustified." *Current Controversies: The Rights of Animals*. San Diego: Greenhaven Press, 1999. *Bookrags*. Web. 2 Nov. 2009.

Coalition to End Primate Experimentation. "Nonhuman Primates Should Not Be Used In Experiments." *Opposing Viewpoints: Animal Experimentation*. San Diego: Greenhaven Press, 2002. Web. 2 Nov. 2009.

Greek, Ray and Jean Swingle. "Animal Testing is Not Essential for Medical Research." *At Issue: Animal Experimentation*. San Diego: Greenhaven Press, 2004. *Bookrags*.Web. 2 Nov. 2009.

Lewis, Katherine. "Animal Experimentation in Education is Unethical." *At Issue: Animal Experimentation*. San Diego: Greenhaven Press, 2000. *Bookrags*. Web. 2 Nov. 2009.

Pardue, Leslie. "Alternatives to Animal Testing Should Be Pursued." *Animal Experimentation*. San Diego: Greenhaven Press, 2000. *Bookrags*. Web. 2 Nov. 2009.

Cultural Identities: Enslavement to Chic

Ashlee Rose Perez

The media controls the basis of American pop culture, which, in turn, determines the standards of the younger generation. What people see on television and in the music industry is likely to be imitated to obtain general acceptance in various social circles. American pop culture has sought to establish a connection between an individual's attire and his/her preferred lifestyle. Some people purposely wear certain items of clothing in order to fit into certain cliques. As a result, people are categorized for the clothes they choose to wear. However, they shouldn't be.

Fashion can serve as a tool of conformity, a weapon of exclusion, or can reflect one's personal enlightenment. It can be used in various ways based on the individual's needs. Joanne Finkelstein, author of *After a Fashion, Slaves of Chic: An A-Z of Consumer Pleasures,* and a professor at Monash University, notes that "an underestimated social force, [fashion] functions effectively not only as an economic colossus but also to engineer social practices. [It is the] interplay of consumer tastes, social habits, and personal identity." What people wear sends signals about what they do, how they do it, and their reasons for doing what they do. However, these messages can be deceptive. For example, someone dressed in a graphic T-shirt passes by; the slogan reads "Vegetarianism & Environmentalism." One might assume that the person is "going veg and going green;" two aspects of that person's life (diet and lifestyle) can already be inferred simply by a glance. However, might all this just be a coincidence? Might this individual be a devout carnivore whose undone laundry has led him or her to borrow a roommate's shirt?
My point exactly.

Clothes are just material objects. Generally speaking (and taking into account variance in quality), the actual labels themselves (from brands that are popularly advertised) are the main difference between one piece of clothing and another. Pop culture has dramatically influenced people's wardrobe and simultaneously tainted individuality. Conformity in a certain clique may make the person feel welcomed and embraced by their decision to partake in certain interests; rebels, on the other hand, may be shunned for their personal discrepancies.

Conforming is not necessarily a bad thing, especially when you're the "new kid on the block." It might even be crucial to a person's life to conform to the codes of a particular clique. People have a need to feel socially accepted by others in order to function properly; acceptance is a part of human nature. Sharing a common fashion is a sure way to identify with a group. One's diet, personal lifestyle, music choices, etc. then follow. For example, adopting the "punk-rock" look was what Greg Graffin, author of "Anarchy in the Tenth Grade," did in his teen years. Only then, did he make music and lifestyle choices. Graffin wanted to fit in with the misfits and found solace among the "punks." Eventually, he partook of their habits, both the good and bad, and observed that some of these lifestyle choices have affected his adult life (Graffin 40). In adhering to "punk" style, Graffin ultimately found himself part of a group with a particular culture. Joanne Finkelstein elaborates on the subject, "Fashion provides a short cut by which we enter another identity and join a subculture that insulates us from contamination by other styles." Sickened by the ubiquitous Californian lifestyle, being "punk" was a form of "insulation" to Graffin. Those who saw Graffin in high school could have made assumptions about his entire way of life based on what he wore. In his case, they would have been correct; he was a walking stereotype.

Not everyone is so transparent, however. As previously mentioned, one can be clad in something out of sheer convenience. I, for one, am an extreme case. My style is my own. I follow not what other's judge to be "in," but rather what I choose to be "fit" for that day. I dress according to my mood, and although I favor the shade of black, I am not what is commonly referred to as "gothic." If the same person were to meet me every day of the week, s/he wouldn't know what to label me as—my style changes from day to day and often to drastic degrees. One day I will dress "girly," with a trendy miniskirt with high-top socks and high heel shoes; the next day will find me in "street style," with large hoop earrings, jeans, and sneakers. By the third day, I may look like a rocker chick covered in chains. People's first impression of me is usually not very informative. If one were to judge me just by my clothing, one would be baffled, wondering whether I'm rebellious or conformist, conservative or radical.

I enjoy being classified as "unclassifiable," to be such is an honor, and I admire others who share this trait such as Gwen Stefani, Madonna, and Christina Aguilera, who are all legends in part because of the unconventional styles they choose to don, as well as their tendency to change them. Their eccentricity marks their uniqueness; they inhibit the media from tainting their individualities by pursuing their own desires regardless of what is taboo to mainstream America. To this day, reporters find it difficult to categorize anyone of the aforementioned stars partly because their fashion choices have made them so unique.

Personality is not something that is tangible; it cannot be bought, sold or advertised as a commodity. Or so I once believed. Because of American pop culture stereotypes, the "fashion industries are deeply implicated in the manufacture of 'personality,'" and feed off consumer needs to assimilate to popular culture (Finkelstein). Almost since birth, we have been trained to absorb the images shown to us on television, in the movies, and in fashion magazines. We have been told to assimilate these images into our everyday lives. The next time you're rummaging through your closet, stop, and think to yourself, "I am choosing what to wear, NOT who to be."

Works Cited

Finkelstein, Joanne. "Chic Theory." Australianhumanistreview.org. n.p. Mar. 1997. Web. 20 Nov. 2008.

Graffin, Greg. "Anarchy in the Tenth Grade." *The Conscious Reader*. 10th ed. Ed. Caroline Shrodes, et al. New York: Pearson/ Longman, 2005: 40-45. Print.

Cheerleading Should Be Considered a Sport
JACQUELINE SIMONSON

There I was lying back down on the floor. All I could feel was pain and the blood dripping down my face onto the raggedy blue mats. At my school, cheerleading was considered an activity and not a regular sport, so we had to practice in the cafeteria with old mats because we couldn't get the funding other sports teams had. My fall occurred during competition season, which meant extra practices and more work for everyone. We were practicing an advanced kick twist toss when I was hurt. A girl fell on me and tore my gums, cracked two of my teeth, split both my lips and my teeth were pushed forward. Maybe if we had better mats and a bigger space to practice in, I wouldn't have been injured; but in order to have those resources, we would have needed to have been considered as participating in a sport.

In spite of what my high school officials thought, cheerleading is clearly a sport. Practices for a competitive team can range from three to five times a week. Then there are workouts cheerleaders must do to stay in top shape. Because a three-minute cheerleading routine includes dances, cheers, and many stunts, a cheerleader must be in good enough shape not to be exhausted by the end of a routine.

Sadly, though, Cheerleaders have been stereotyped because people don't know what cheerleaders really do. "Cheerleading is not a sport because it's typically for neurotic blondes with disorders of both the eating and attention deficit variety," argues blog poster Bill Lumbergh. Another blog poster agrees, adding, "cheerleaders are like jockstraps, they are athletic supporters not athletes" ("Cheerleading").

These statements are not arguments because they provide no logical reasons as to why cheerleading is not a sport. Posters such as Lumbergh are just attacking the cheerleader image, which is based on stereotypes. In many people's minds, cheerleading consists of pretty girls who exist solely to cheer on the boys. However, cheerleading isn't about standing on the sidelines. Most cheerleading teams have rules that all members must have a certain grade point average and be in excellent physical condition in order to participate in the program. Cheering at varsity games is now considered a practice time for competition. In these competitions, cheerleaders must perform complex routines, and those who compete for national titles risk great injury.

To see if cheerleading really is a sport, there must be a clear definition of what a sport is. The criteria are that it must be a competition, it must have athletes (someone who is skilled at the game), and it must be an activity requiring skill or physical ability that lends itself to competition (Galletti). Obviously, cheerleaders do compete at competitions, but this does not automatically make cheerleading a sport. The American Association of Cheerleading Coaches and Advisors (AACCA) argue that although cheerleading is physical activity, it is not a sport. They argue that to be a sport, an activity's primary goal must be to compete. "Cheerleading in its current format, does not meet the criteria. The primary purpose is not competition, but that of raising school unity through leading the crowd at athletic functions" (AACCA). Therefore, this group of cheerleading coaches says that they consider cheerleading only an athletic activity.

As a cheerleader, I believe that cheerleading does share many of the elements that make up other competitive sports. It definitely involves intense physical training. The skills in learning to tumble require a cheerleader to perform standing back flips and full layouts as well as performing them in the air. A cheerleader must also have the strength to lift girls in the air, and the girls in the air must have the strength to hold their own weight and control their bodies to avoid injuries. Cheerleaders do go to competitions in which all teams strive to be the best. Points are given to teams with the best technique, difficulty, and creativity. There are also rules that must be followed to participate just like in many other sports. There is strategy because in the case that something goes wrong on a competition mat, the team must work together to fix the problem. When doing complicated pyramids, for example, it is so easy for a hand to slip and cause many girls to fall.

Cheerleading is much more physically intense than people may think. "According to the National Center for Catastrophic Sport Injury Research, cheerleading is the number 1 cause of serious sports injuries to women" ("Girls'"). Cheerleaders do not wear any type of protection or padding. They are taught at an early age that it is not acceptable not to finish a routine. This means that even if you are kicked in the face and have a broken nose, you finish what you started. New data shows cheerleading accounted for 66.7 percent of all female sports catastrophic injuries, compared to past estimates of 59.4 percent ("Girls'"). The most common injuries were arm and leg strains and sprains, but 3.5 percent of the cases involved head injuries. These injuries have increased due to cheerleaders trying stunts that are more difficult and not having the proper training. Not being considered a sport means that it is just an activity. Activities don't have certain rules, regulations, or particular training to prepare for stunts. The coaches also don't need to undergo standardized training if it is not a sport. Some teams may not even have to have a coach at all. Being considered a sport could prevent many of the injuries that occur frequently in cheerleading.

If people would stop to realize that cheerleaders aren't just a bunch of so-called bimbos in short skirts hopping around, maybe cheerleaders would be able to be considered a sport. If it were considered a sport, cheerleading would become much safer. Cheerleading follows all the guidelines to be considered a sport as teams are judged for their stunts, dances, cheers, and tumbling. Cheerleaders are definitely athletes, and they practice and work hard at their goals.

Works Cited

American Association of Cheerleading Coaches and Advisors. "Facts." *aacca.org*. American Association of Cheerleading Coaches and Advisors, n.d. Web. 2 Dec. 2008.

Galletti, Karla S. *Cheerleading: The Sport for Athletes.* Karla S. Galleti, n.d. Web. 30 Nov. 2008.

"Girls' Most Dangerous Sport: Cheerleading." *LiveScience.com*, Livescience. n.d. Web. 30 Nov. 2008.

Lumberg, Bill. "Cheerleading Is Not a Sport." *Sportsfilter.com* n.p. n.d. Web. 2 Dec. 2008.

What's Wrong With This Picture?
Genesis Maria Reyes

I remember the first time Osborne kissed me. It was the summer of 2009, and the sun's rays beat down on us harder than the tidal waves that crashed on the beach beside us. It was simple, quick, and, for the most part, on the cheek, but I wouldn't have had it any other way. He smelled fishy and the hairs on his nose tickled a bit as he leaned in. Nonetheless, it was absolutely a memorable experience. It was the moment in time that everything inside me changed. That's the type of impression Osborne the sea lion can leave on people.

Born and raised in the New York Aquarium, located on Surf Avenue by Coney Island, Osborne is a product of the Wildlife Conservation Society's mission to save wildlife all over world, as well as help humans interact with them in an educational manner. The Wildlife Conservation Society (WCS) is an organization stationed all over the globe to help the quality of our wildlife by hosting campaigns and projects as well as by running educational facilities such as zoos and aquariums. They help us understand why it is important to conserve and what actions we must take to protect wildlife around us. So why does it make any sense that Governor Patterson wants to cut them out of New York's state's 2010 budget completely? The Wildlife Conservation Society should keep its funding because the organization is educational, financially beneficial, and, most importantly, vital to the animals who reside in their living museums.

The current economic downturn in the State of New York has hit everyone like a herd of stampeding elephants. Budget cuts across the state map have resulted in employees being laid off from their jobs. Employees of the WCS have been no exception. In fact, the WCS has been battling Patterson's budget proposals since 2009 when he anticipated a 55 percentage budget cut to 76 zoos, botanical gardens, and aquariums ("NY Governor") and now he wants to cut them completely from next year's budget. Complete cuts are ridiculous; they pose horrible threats to city zoos and nature preserves.

The Wildlife Conservation Society has struggled immensely, trying to keep up with budget deficits by laying off staff whom they can afford to lose. In addition, the WCS had to cut many of its educational programs that keep the community aware of issues. Eliminating programs like these will eventually lead to a future where fewer and fewer city and state residents possess knowledge about wildlife. Karl Lauby of the New York Botanical Garden notes that WCS facilities and programs are very much responsible for "inspiring future generations of environmentalists who will care for the fragile plants and wildlife of the Earth" (qtd. in "NY Governor"). Our future generation's knowledge of wildlife will deteriorate if no one is there to carry out the legacy of this organization.

One of the most notorious stories of an educational exhibit being closed down happened in April of 2009 right in the heart of Southern Boulevard in the Bronx. The Bronx Zoo closed one of its oldest exhibits, The World of Darkness (known for its bats), due to a $15 million dollar cut. Bats, porcupines, primates, including Lemurs and night monkeys had to be shipped to other zoos (Goldenberg). The story appeared in several newspapers as well as the *New York Post* who titled the story "Wild-Fired by the Zoo." Now that the exhibit is gone, how will children and adults learn that bats are an important part of our ecosystem and that they are in decline due to human fear and persecution (Boleky)? This is the type of information we, as a community, miss out on when programs are shut down. Our knowledge of animals is at stake when they need us the most.

Now, there are proposals for additional closures. Mayor Bloomberg has proposed that both the Prospect Park and Queens zoos, two historic institutions, be closed. In a newspaper interview with Debbie Officer from the *Amsterdam News*, Dr. Steven E. Sanderson, President and CEO of WCS stated, "This is not a budgetary exercise. This is the lives of 211 people, the displacement of thousands of animals and the dismantling of the world's largest and most distinguished network of urban wildlife parks" (Officer 35). This statement poses the question on every animal lover's mind: How does one lay off animals? You don't; you simply ship them off to another place, which might sound like a resolution, but it is not. Animals will suffer as a result of the stresses that come from trying to adapt to a new habitat elsewhere. The abrupt closing of two zoos is unnecessary and, frankly, immoral when one considers the stress the animals will face just to make the budget look better.

Mayor Bloomberg and Governor Patterson are overlooking the fact that The WCS actually brings in money to New York City. In addition to educating children and families all over the city, the WCS is a financial treasure. In the 2009 *New York Times* article "Proposed Budget Shuts out Zoos, Aquariums and Gardens," Dr. Sanderson appears again, this time pointing out that the Bronx Zoo and the New York Aquarium alone draw 2.7 million annual visitors and generate $300 million for New York's economy every year (Bagli). That's just two wildlife parks. Imagine the income that all five parks bring in every year (the five parks being the Bronx Zoo, Central Park Zoo, Prospect Park Zoo, Queens Zoo, and the New York Aquarium). Budgets cuts like the ones WCS has been experiencing imply that the state has failed to recognize these impressive economic contributions.

Interestingly, the only WCS facility at this point in time that is being provided with state funds is the New York Aquarium. The Bloomberg administration has set aside $41 million dollars to create two massive shark tanks for more than 30 sharks. In addition to those plans, there will also be a variety of new exhibits that connect the boardwalk to another major street near Coney Island (Bagli). However, this was no act of generosity from Bloomberg.

The "Sea Change" plan, as Bloomberg calls it, seems to be a refreshing idea, but what's wrong with this picture? In 2008, the Bloomberg administration actually rejected a similar plan that the Wildlife Society proposed because it "failed to transform the building's exterior and create a more engaging link to the Boardwalk and Surf Avenue" (Bagli). Intense renovation plans have hit Coney Island in an attempt to make it a more tourist- and economic-friendly area. As it's widely known, the New York Aquarium rests on the boardwalk, which ties Brighton Beach and Coney Island. From a marketer's point of view, it wouldn't be aesthetically pleasing if the facility right next to an upscale Coney Island was run down. The massive tanks will be constructed to be seen from the Coney Island boardwalk. In the end, what is missing from Bloomberg's Sea Change plan is any mention of the well-being of the Aquarium's animals. From his point of view, the Aquarium gets the money only because its renovation will enhance Coney Island. If Coney Island were not undergoing gentrification, what would have happened to residents of the Aquarium, animals like Osborne?

The Wildlife Conservation Society contributes to the City of New York in a variety of ways, from adding to our economy as well as providing an education about our ecosystem. In desperate times, when New York City is suffering from an economic recession, pollution, and the threat of terrorist attacks, we need to come together to stop Governor Patterson from slowly taking away one of the most positive organizations the city has to offer. We must defend our zoos and aquariums because they are a part of where we live. We also need to remember that the animals in our zoos need our protection. Just as the WCS's mission statement says, the continued existence of the Wildlife Conservation Society, its city parks and educational projects are "essential to the integrity of life on Earth."

Works Cited

"About Us: Our Mission Statement." *Wildlife Conservation Society,* Wildlife Conservation Society, Bronx, New York (1985). Web. 2 May 2010.

Bagli, Charles. "Aquarium to Renovate With Giant Shark Tanks." *New York Times.com, New York Times.* 16 Sept. 2009. Web. 15 Apr. 2010.

Boleky, Vaughan. "The Importance of Bat Houses." Organization for Bat Conservation, Michigan 2006. Web. 24 April 2010.

Goldenberg, Sally. "Wild-Fired by the Zoo: Cuts will Oust Hundreds of Bronx Beasties." *New York Post.* NYP Holdings, Inc. 24 Apr. 2009. Web. 15 Apr. 2010.

"NY Governor to Cut Zoo and Aquarium Budgets 55%." *Mongabay.com.* Rhett Butler. 13. Jan. 2009. Web. 16 Apr. 2010.

Officer, Debbie A. "Mayor's Budget will Hurt Children, and Their Furry Friends." *New York Amsterdam News*: 94.17 2-3 (2003) Web. 25 Mar. 2010.

Pogrebin, Robin. "Proposed Budget Shuts Out Zoos, Aquariums and Gardens." *New York Times.com, New York Times.* 21 Jan. 2010 Web. 23 Mar. 2010.

Video Gaming: A New Form of Story Telling
BRIAN GARRITANO

Alexandra Roivas travels to her grandfather's house in Rhode Island after he died an unexpected and violent death. Frustrated with the local police department's inability to make any progress solving the murder, she begins to investigate the mansion herself and finds a long history of occult and magic stretching through her family's ancestry into ancient times. While this probably sounds like the teaser for a new book or horror movie, it is actually the introduction to a videogame. Many people believe that the content of video games is immature and violent, but the complex storylines and mature themes of many video games often surprise people.

Most people in contemporary America view video games as unnecessarily violent or childish and mistakenly assume that video games exist solely as entertainment, exhibit no values, and have no impact, except an improved reaction time (Bartlett 96-102). While some games, such as *Grand Theft Auto III* by Rockstar Games, perpetuate this stereotype, they may also act as a form of stress relief for many players. Currently there is a wide variety of games in the video gaming community that contain mature content, addressing universal themes in an entertaining way without resorting to excessive violence. Compared to literature, the *Grand Theft Auto* series is the video game equivalent of a modern thriller: exciting and popular, but of little substance. Yet only a small percentage of video games are violent, while a large number of games exist for older, more mature players. In addition, there is a recurring motif of violence in storytelling, from horror books to movies like *Saw V*. However, these well-known horror books and films are typically viewed as more respectable than video games. Video games are criticized because they are new and had humble beginnings. While they have matured, public opinion about them has not. Video games have a lot to offer because they are contemporary and their electronic medium is both innovative and allows for more interaction.

The majority of video game companies consider each new game to be a massive undertaking as a creative project. Companies often hire professionally trained composers, such as Nobuo Uematsu, to make soundtracks as well as multiple artists as concept designers to form the world, scenery, and characters of the game. In addition, voice actors give life to the characters, while professional writers create the plot and background stories and develop characters. This shows that video game professionals take their work seriously. In the video game industry, a lot of time and money goes into creating a high quality product. Furthermore, video games have a rating system, ranging from "E" for everyone to "M" for mature, and M-rated video games often have little to no violence and no nudity, but address a number of mature themes such as the death of loved ones, substance addiction, or political matters. Yet, most critics object to video games, and say that M-rated video games are simply violent and pornographic, such as *Grand Theft Auto*. Unfortunately, they criticize the medium unjustly and create a bad reputation for all video games based on the flaws of a few. These critics focus the one or two worst examples, and refuse to view anything else objectively. Video games are unique in that, the story is accented by acting, music, and an interactive quality that is not present in most forms of media.

A powerful example of the complex stories in videogames is *Final Fantasy 6* developed by Square Enix. The game focuses on the storyline and character development, fused by tactical turn-based battles in which the player selects moves from a variety of options, choosing the most beneficial one given the situation. An explicit example of the game's mature content occurs in the second half of the game, as the game's villain, a sociopath named General Kefka Palazzo who usurps his emperor's throne, and seizes magical power from three ancient statues. The context of the game has significant rising tension and this move makes sense, but his action devastates the world. The female character, Celes Chere, awakes a year later to find the world in ruins, most of its population wiped out, and the ground infertile. Trapped on a small island, she is devastated when her father passes away shortly after she awakens from her coma. Celes is then alone and, hopes shattered, attempts to commit suicide. She fails to do so, and the game goes on, but she learns hope and sets out to find her missing friends. This dramatic plot, while inappropriate for some age groups, has universal themes like the power of hope. Celes learns to have hope, realizing that she should not have attempted suicide. This is just one example of the mature and complex themes in videogames, which are too often overlooked.

Unlike books, videogames succeed as a medium in part because they offer alternate structures for telling a story. The game *Eternal Darkness* (Nintendo) combines its plot structure with a unique interactive format and focuses on an ancient undead sorcerer trying to revive a dead God at the new millennia. The game spans across multiple centuries with different characters, each adding a piece to the puzzle; it finally ends with the aforementioned character, Alexandra Roivas, who figures out the mystery and moves to stop the ancient demon god from rising. The player acts as Alexandra throughout the game, finding pages of an ancient tome, where the player then plays as previous owners of the tome in a non-linear narrative. The narrative also takes a tone of historical fiction, which could then introduce the player to new genres they would otherwise have missed, while maintaining elements of the psychological horror genre. The story alternates between the distant past and the present. As a comparison, the structure is similar to Mary Shelley's frame story in the novel *Frankenstein*.

Most interestingly, *Eternal Darkness* has various special effects and tools that add more layers of complexity. There is a meter indicative of the current character's sanity as he or she endures absurd and horrifying obstacles. As the level of sanity decreases, the character and player start to hallucinate. The game will first emit strange sounds like a woman crying or present visual effects like making the room crooked. As the meter further decreases, the game creates more extensive illusions, such as a head floating on the screen and quoting Edgar Allen Poe, or the word "MUTE" might appear on the screen, eliminating all sound. Many of the hallucinations intentionally blur the line between reality and the game, having an adverse effect on the player's state of mind. For instance, with the above illusion, whoever is playing may reach to turn up the television's volume, thinking someone sat on the remote, when really the game muted itself as a trick. Other illusions include a blue error screen, or a mass of realistic bugs crawling onto the screen one by one. The game gives a sensory experience to the player, affecting his or her sight and feelings. It psychologically unnerves the player in a way that most mediums are incapable of doing. It interacts directly with the player, and things that happen to the player's character happen to the player. This lends itself to the atmosphere more than most books or movie do, since the game doesn't rely on the player imagining its horrors; it surrounds the player in them. The game makes the player constantly question what is real, with no way for them to differentiate illusion from the game's intentional peculiarities such as playing as a character who slowly decays into a zombie. This creates unease in a very new way that is seldom, if ever, accomplished in books or a movies. Certainly, the versatile software of videogames allows for story telling in new ways. Games such as *Eternal Darkness* have complex plots that add to their depth and unique ways of presenting a narrative.

Video games employ a wide variety of methods to tell stories and develop their themes. *Eternal Darkness* includes a structure of multiple people passing down an ancient tome, and the setting, music, and interactive features all heighten the experience. Other games such as *Final Fantasy* share more common narrative formats with other genres such as books or movies, and have well-developed characters who engage the player with their realism. Surprisingly, video games are a relevant new means of storytelling; they address universal themes in new ways. As Rohrer agrees, they are one worth experiencing (160-188). Now that advancements in technology have allowed storytelling to become a more interactive medium, people should not presume that all video games are a violent indulgence.

Works Cited

Bartlett, Christopher P., et al. "The Effect of Violent and Non-Violent Computer Games on Cognitive Performance." *Computers in Human Behavior*. Jan. 2009 25.1: 96-102. *Academic Search Premier*. Web. 1 Dec.

Eternal Darkness. Kyoto, Japan: Nintendo, 2002.

Final Fantasy VI. Shibuya, Tokyo, Japan: Square Enix, 1994.

Grand Theft Auto III. New York, NY: Rockstar Games, 2001.

Rohrer, Jason. "Toward a Future in Which Pixels and Code and Computers Will Make You Cry and Feel and Love." *Esquire* Dec. 2008, Vol. 150 Issue 6, p160-188. *Academic Search Premier*. Web. 1 Dec. 2008.

Creative Writing / Art

Creative work encompasses multiple genres: poetry and verse, fiction, and visual media, such as graphic narrative. As with formal and informal essays, the style and the substance are related—but creative work often foregrounds this relationship—or uses the form to *add* meaning to the content—that would not be possible to do using other means.

Self Poem

ELIZABETH PETERSEN

It's hard to describe the indescribable.
It's near impossible to describe yourself.
There are just too many adjectives.
Too many ways to describe oneself . . .
She's thin, short, and shy.
Then you see her laughing.
Blink and she's gone.
Walking very, very fast.
She's serious and determined.
She doesn't know herself.
But she does.
Facts are what she knows.
She's loyal to those facts.
Very, very loyal.
She's regimented.
She has to be.
No choice in that.
But she's also lazy.
She's intellectual.
She loves learning.
She's scared.
Of a lot of things.
Someone once said,
She has quiet confidence.
So why is it,
She doesn't always have it?
She's frustrated.
Frustrated a lot.
She's a perfectionist.
She hates things.
But doesn't like even more.
She loves things.
But likes even more.
She's weird.
She's proud of her weirdness.
She's confused.
She doesn't like this.
Because of the simple fact.
She doesn't know herself.

Finding Love

NOËL A. COLEMAN

"My Lord?"

The words were whispered, and echoed still against the rock walls.

The answering silence gripped my heart, and my steps grew quick. I could not run, I knew, a Lady does not run.

The castle was quiet, it was a rare occurrence.

The floor seemed suddenly uncertain, but I increased my pace.

I inquired once more for my sweet Love, hoping he would respond. But the corridor was long and barren.

Tables stood on either side, and a tapestry hung from the wall. I recalled it as a wedding gift, the thought bringing a smile to my lips.

The clicking of my shoes reverberated against the stones. The echo came in pace with my own heart.

It filled my chest; the experience was dizzying.

I slowed my pace, worrying what a servant might think.

The Queen was running. She looked frantic, a horrible leader.

I imagined my King's reaction.

He would simply laugh it off, finding it adorable I had worried so for him. His lips would gently grace my forehead, my cheek, my hand.

I can hear his words, "don't worry," and the calm sweeping over me. But he was not there, and so I worried.

The corridor twisted, and I whispered once more for my love. I had awoken alone, the bed cold and unfamiliar.

The worry was slowly melting away, as the annoyance arose. The library was ahead, my last place to look.

I opened the heavy doors to enter our private world of words.

And there he sat.

A candle burning sweetly in the darkness.

The flames licked the air, and shadows danced upon his face. His hair was pulled back, tucked behind an ear haphazardly. He looked up slowly, as if I had woken him from a dream.

My annoyance melted away, his eyes smiling upon my entrance. I stepped carefully, but the echoes still vibrated within my chest. I crossed the room to his side, and smiled with mock anger . . .

But he saw through my act and his soft laughter destroyed my resolve.

My King carefully placed his book upon a table, and took my hands in his.

He pulled me down, sliding me into his lap. His arms curled around my sides, a perfect fit.

"My Queen," he whispered softly into my hair, and graced me with a kiss. "You were gone . . ."

My reason for the frantic searching sounded weak.

"I am never gone."

In a moment, I was whole again.

As the memories of lifetimes past, present and future returned. He slowly lifted me to my feet, moving with grace and ease. "This is not a time for you to worry so . . ." his words drifted off, And the knowledge of my condition passed between us.

He began to guide me gently back towards our chambers.

The air filled with whispered promises of ending nightly departures. I smiled gently, and hoped we would not awaken the castle.

His arm rested lightly across my shoulders and the thought disappeared. His closeness created a reaction, and our unborn child gave a start.

I was filled with elation.

This was my perfection, my home, my whole self.

I had found my other half, and was allowed to truly be with him. A prayer to my God went up from my heart in thankfulness.

We passed the tapestry, and I saw a familiar smile on my King's face.

This was what finding love meant.

My Apology (*after A Clockwork Orange*)
FRANCISCO ALVARENGA

I have been a bad boy, I know it. I look back on what I've done to so many people and, though I have been cured by the Ludovico Technique, I still feel a bit nauseous. I was terrible, and now I offer my apology to any and all who will accept it. I cannot say that I have found God, as many who have been in prison say they do, but I have found the courage to admit my wrongdoings. I announce now, with all of you as my witnesses, that I have turned away from my past and will begin a life of goodness and morality. Put simply, I have grown up. Perhaps there are those of you who do not know who I am or what I have done. To answer the former, I am Alex DeLarge, a citizen of the fair city of London. To answer the latter it will take a bit more words and time, so I pray that you are all patient enough to read my story to the end. I suppose the best place to start is just a few weeks before I was sent to prison, for it is then that I performed my worst acts.

To society, I am summed up with just one word, a criminal; of course people I've come in contact with refer to me with a series of curse words. Being near me was not something most people wished for, save for my friends, who listened obediently to every word I said. Including me, there were four of us—me, Pete, Georgie, and Dim. Many a night we found ourselves sitting in the milk-bar, making up our minds about what to do that night. I see now that whatever it was we decided to do, someone would get hurt, whether emotionally or physically. Our favorite nighttime events were robbery, vandalism, and rape. Perhaps this is why no one cared for us much. My friends and I were certain we were having the same nocturnal fun all other teenagers in London were having, and please believe me when I say it was fun, we lived for it.

We lived like this for years. The police hassled me constantly, but they never caught me or my friends in the act. Witness accounts were not enough to break my rehearsed lies. As far as I was concerned, these police officers were just a nuisance that I would have to thwart again and again. Of course, they all knew I was responsible for the pillaging, especially as the ringleader of the group, but they never had enough evidence, and until they found enough, I would continue to have my fun.

There are two nights in particular that would eventually come back to haunt me. The first was on a rather enjoyable night where my friends and I stole a car and gave it a little spin through London. We enjoyed the ride and listened to the beautiful sounds of Beethoven's genius compositions on the radio until we came across an isolated house in the countryside. Lights were on inside, so we did what we felt was only polite and gave the couple inside some company. We beat the man until he was all nice and bloody and made him watch as we all took turns giving his wife the old in-out. With the police yearning to find more excuses to knock on our doors, we wore masks to avoid detection. Afterwards, we headed back to the city, and relaxed in the milk-bar, chatting about the night over a nice glass of milk. It was while we sat and talked that Dim, being named such for his stupidity, harmed a woman for singing the lovely sounds of opera too loudly. I gave Dim a right punch in the gut for interrupting such beautiful music. He groaned, but did not fight back. My friends knew not to fight with me. I was boss.

The following day, after skipping school and having fun with two girls I met in a record store, I met up with my friends again. This is when Georgie showed signs of wanting to be our gang's leader. He challenged me to rob from a rich old woman who lives alone with her cats.

Were it my idea, I would have enjoyed the task, but since it was a test of my manhood and leadership I grew furious. I slashed Georgie and Dim with a knife for it, then I offered them a drink at the milk-bar, to show we were still friends. After having our drinks, my gang was in no mood to do much of anything that night, but I had had no fun yet, and I insisted we go through with stealing from the wealthy lady. At her house, I entered through the second story window, and fought with the woman inside, and then I knocked her to the floor to stop her from calling those menacing police. I found out to my dismay, however, that Dim, Georgie and Pete called the police anyway to have me caught. They did not want me as a leader or a friend. I had no way of escaping; I was trapped.

Naturally I was in trouble now for having been caught trespassing. The police tortured me 'til I confessed to everything, the entire lot— stealing, beating, raping, everything up to the night with the old lady. I made sure to include my so-called friends in it, too. The police seemed pleased. Even more so later that night when they woke me and told me the old lady had died. I must have hit her a bit harder than I had thought. Now I was in real trouble. I had done everything a criminal could do, and I was still only fifteen.

So off to State Jail I went. I spent much time speaking with the chaplain, learning about God and roads to salvation. I didn't believe much of it, but I wanted to believe there was a way out of jail, or at least out of the reality of jail. Then came the day I thought to be glorious when I heard news of a new procedure that took a criminal and made him a good, law-abiding citizen. It was a way out of the prison, so I volunteered myself. After hearing of my past acts, everyone seemed quite pleased to experiment on me, so they strapped me to a chair before a grand screen and gave me drugs to which nausea is the only intended result. I was forced to watch hours and hours worth of violence, so that by seeing such events while under the sickness of the drugs, I would feel sick by the mere thought of violence. There was something I realized hours into the procedure, however, that terrified me. The clips of violence were accompanied by a soundtrack of classical music! I screamed for them to stop the music. It was a sin for them to destroy my love of music, too, but the doctors did not oblige, stating that it was for my own good.

After two weeks of the same routine, I was shown off to a group of men who watched me keenly. Oh my brothers, they presented your fair and humble narrator with women who I would have given the old in-out to right there on the stage, but as soon as the notion crawled into my brain I was overwhelmed by sickness. The officials saw that I was indeed unable to commit any act of violence, no matter how small, and let me go back into society. I had become a clockwork orange, brothers, an organism as ordinary as an orange on the outside, yet mechanical and routine on the inside. In other words, I had lost my free will.

Once in the outside world again, I discovered two things. The first was that my dear friend Georgie was dead. He assumed leadership during my absence and picked a fight with a man a bit stronger than he had thought. The second was just how many people hated me. As I wandered back home, I came across old men, teenage women and everyone else I had hurt during my period of violence. Now they wanted to get their revenge, and I was unable, thanks to the Ludovico Technique, to defend myself. How embarrassing it was to have the crap knocked out of me by old men in a library! To add insult to injury, when I arrived home, my parents had rented out my room. They had replaced me! I was defenseless, and now homeless.

I walked through London, trying to decide what to do. I decided I would listen to music, the one thing that could always elate me. But upon my arrival to the record store I heard the sounds of the wonderful Beethoven and instantly felt sick to my stomach. I had forgotten the monsters at the state jail had taken my love of music, too. With nothing to give me any hope in the future, I planned to take my life. Now, obviously I did not succeed, for how would I be able to rewrite this account if I had? In fact, I couldn't even think about it— my treatment had made me incapable of committing any acts of violence, even to myself. I found myself wandering the streets again, this time accompanied by another group of people I had harmed back in my violent days. They beat me senseless and called the police. As it turns out, my old friend Dim was one of the officers. He apparently was still angry about the slash I gave him all those years ago and took me to the countryside in his police car and, instead of helping me, beat me up too. I had never been physically accosted so many times in one day. Dim left me to die in the middle of nowhere, but for whatever reason God did not see it as my time. I found the energy to walk far enough to find an isolated house. Little did I know this was the house my friends and I had invaded years ago where we violated that woman and made her husband watch.

The husband opened the door and welcomed me into his home. He had no idea who I was, for I had been wearing a mask the first time I had been inside. He treated me well, helped me recover, and I was grateful. Unfortunately, I was not careful with my words, and the man soon came to realize who I was. He did nothing to me at first, so I was never aware of his new knowledge. He brought me to his attic where he locked me in and began to play my once favorite music, the lovely sounds of Beethoven. Of course, I could not bear to listen to it my brothers, and after suffering for more than ten minutes, I ran towards the window and jumped out.

Again, my hopes of dying were dashed. I awoke in a hospital bed, where I learned the events that had taken place during my unconsciousness. The man who tortured me with music was sentenced to jail for unlawfully using me as a pawn in his game to destroy the government; apparently he knew of my treatment and its effects, and wanted to show the world what terrors the government had caused by exposing me to the Ludovico Technique. In addition, I was told that, for fear of receiving bad publicity, the government reversed the effects of the treatment, curing me of the terrible symptoms. I was cured! I was cured and had my free will back again! Life was as it should be.

After being released from the hospital, I made up for lost time. I gathered a new gang of friends and roamed the streets at night, stealing and beating all over again. But, alas, it was not the same. I did not feel the joy I once did at the sight of blood. I was becoming bored with violence. I began to think of my future—my career, my wife, and my kids if I had any. Would they be as mischievous as I was in my youth? I decided it was best to plan for the days ahead, and so I gave up my days of mayhem. Now I am here today, issuing an apology to all those I harmed before and after my treatment. I have learned the error of my ways and wish only to be forgiven and begin my life anew. I am cured, Oh my brothers, I am cured!

A Girl and Her Young Boy

TAYLOR BROOKS STEINBERG

A girl and a young boy turned off the main road
ignoring the yellow, warning,   "dead end."
      The girl lit a cigarette. The boy said, "No thanks,"
        still savoring the taste from supper.

The pair inched closer as the road narrowed
      turning repetitive steps into sweet, **hand-locked, rolling bliss**.

And so no mind was paid to the disappearing   sidewalk or the gravel,
      as it dissolved to

             d

                  u

                     s

                         t,

    then back into dirt.

    And though the wooded area had laid   dead ahead for some time,
it still did not flinch the two, or even encourage the slightest peek to passed side-streets.
Their heads were fastened forward | toward the looming forest, as they remained intact with
    hand-locked, rolling bliss.
    But soon it really didn't matter, where the attention was devoted,
cause their peripherals no longer caught glimpses of Manheim Avenue and North Front Street.
    They only saw what was left.

      A landscape of trees
        capturing
        the sunlight.

Untitled

Jason Weiss

Ever catch an artist mid-birth?
I did once.

I found a rush of Blush
And a glazing smile.

I felt my throat
Well up.

How honest.

Wintry Lament

BRIAN GARRITANO

Wintry wastelands
excite the child who is ready
to make his mark in the snow.

First, he carves angels, then builds snowmen
to tell the tales of his day.
Yet he is naïve and unaware.

Flurries descend and life persists as
the boy explores and climbs.
Soon he desires a place to rest.

Glacial reflections increase
in frequency, in hue. He presses on
through the snow, up the hill.

Stopping, he sees
the endless frozen seas.
The snow covers him.

The marks he made vanish.

An Audible Virtue
SIMEON YOUNGMANN

Nervously

set-up

and fine tuned

to concert A

Anticipation climbed to soapbox

and set free

Though quietly kept in position by memory.